I0085018

THOUGHT CATALOG BOOKS

Awesomeness

Awesomeness

An Amateur Potpourri of a How-to Guide

ANDREW SYRIOS

Thought Catalog Books

Brooklyn, NY

THOUGHT CATALOG BOOKS

Copyright © 2016 by Andrew Syrios

All rights reserved. Published by Thought Catalog Books, a division of The Thought & Expression Co., Williamsburg, Brooklyn. Founded in 2010, Thought Catalog is a website and imprint dedicated to your ideas and stories. We publish fiction and non-fiction from emerging and established writers across all genres. For general information and submissions: manuscripts@thoughtcatalog.com.

First edition, 2016

ISBN 978-0692678138

10 9 8 7 6 5 4 3 2 1

Cover photography by © Daniela Cuevas

Contents

Part V. Money and Business

Introduction

Awesomeness…

Undoubtedly, the goal of every red-blooded human being. But how does one achieve this laudable state of being? That is the question this book will attempt to answer.

Through much reading as well as personal trial and error, I believe I have found a series of practical steps to increase one's own awesomeness. Wherever your current awesomeness-o-meter is currently stalled at, these steps can push the dial in the right direction. They sure have helped me increase mine (although, many would argue it was lodged so low to begin with that my current state is still not particularly impressive). Regardless, I hope this book will serve you well in your admirable quest to attain the awesomeness you so rightly deserve.

Part 1

Productivity

1

Weekly Goals

Human beings are a goal oriented species. There is just something about having concrete, specific goals that staves off procrastination. And the shorter the time span the better. Weekly goals or something close to that (maybe even daily) are the best. Slacker-productivity expert Timothy Ferris notes this in in hugely popular book *The Four Hour Workweek* saying,

> *I'm not a big believer in long-term planning and far-off goals... The variables change too much and in-the-future distance becomes and excuse for postponing action.*[1]

Don't get me wrong, yearly goals are fine, I have those too and so should you. But think about how many New Years Resolutions are actually followed through on. Meh, forget thinking about it, I'll just tell you. According to a study by the University of Scranton, a thoroughly pathetic 8 percent of New Year's resolutions are actually achieved.[2]

The problem is that when you have 365 days to accomplish something, it's a lot easier to simply say "well, I'll take today

---

1. Timothy Ferris, *The 4-Hour Workweek*, Crown Publishers, Copyright 2007, Pg. 59
2. University of Scranton, *Journal of Clinical Psychology*, New Years Resolution Statistics, January 26th, 2015

off and take care of this in one of the other 364 days." One day then turns into two, two into three, etc.

So what I do is list out my weekly goals on a white board over my bed. I put things like "finish book," "learn new song on guitar," "finish gathering documents for refinance," and off I go. Then I cross each item off as I get them done and at the end of the week I tally up my score. Then the next week, I try to beat my last score. It's basically a little game I play that takes advantage of our naturally competitive instincts to actually be very productive.

And it's not just me; there is empirical evidence to support this. A study from Dominican University comparing those who wrote down their goals versus those that just thought about them concluded,

> *The positive effect of written goals was supported: Those who wrote their goals accomplished signifi-cantly more than those who did not write their goals.* [6.44 to 4.28][3]

And while the study didn't say anything about having such goals prominently displayed, it's well known that the squeaky wheel gets the grease. I am quite certain that having your goals staring you in the face every morning, noon and night on a whiteboard (or something like that) across from your bed drives the point home all the more.

It should also be noted that the study found those who shared their goals and gave progress reports to a friend for

3. *Goals Research Study*, Dominican University, Pg. 3, September 2009

support (or competition) were even more effective. Goals are useless if there's no method of accountability. Goals without accountability are just wishes. The whiteboard across from your bed acts as a form of accountability from yourself. Bringing a friend or family member into the equation adds another element of accountability.

And therein lies the crux of the matter. Goals become attainable when we structure our lives to be accountable to them. This is why short term goals (perhaps in the service of a longer term goal) are so much more effective than long term goals; because we don't have time to put them off and thereby are held more accountable. The same goes for prominently displaying them and getting someone else involved.

Hold yourself accountable to your goals ladies and gentlemen.

2

The Brilliance of Single-Tasking

Multitasking is myth.

Yes, it is widely considered to be a critical skill in today's frantic workplace. Indeed, almost every resume that crosses my desk states that one of the person's many skills is that he or she is a great "multitasker."

My eyes have come to roll at the sight of such "skills" as I long ago reached the conclusion that there are two types of people in this world; bad multitaskers and horrible multitaskers. Gary Keller provides a great analysis of this in his short book *The One Thing*. As he notes,

> *Every time we try to do two or more things at once, we're simply dividing up our focus and dumbing down all of the outcomes in the process. [And to] Bounce between one activity and another you lose time as your brain reorients to the new task. Those milliseconds add up. Researchers estimate that we lose 28 percent of an average workday to multitasking ineffectiveness.*[1]

1. Gary Keller, *The One Thing*, Bard Press, 4/1/2013, Pg. 50

Thus, Keller accurately describes multitasking as "one of the great myths of our time." Perhaps someday I will see one of those resumes more accurately state that the applicant is "great at wasting time by switching from one task to another before finishing the first one."

Personally speaking, a while back I finally made it a major goal of mine to not multitask. Since then, my productivity has increased dramatically. In particular, the projects that "I can just never get back to" don't seem to be around much anymore. Said projects either get finished, or don't get started in the first place. So I have come to call this process single-tasking.

Single-tasking focuses the brain on finishing things. Our brains just don't really multitask, no matter how much we would like them to or how much we try to force them to. Instead, when someone attempts to multitask, his or her brain just goes back and forth between the two separate tasks and is unable to focus on either. This leads to frustration or a feeling of being overwhelmed which then leads to procrastination. Or perhaps we should call it zero-tasking.

Indeed, *Wikipedia's* entry on the subject sums up the research on multitasking quite well,

> *Since the 1990s, experimental psychologists have started experiments on the nature and limits of human multitasking. It has been shown multitasking is not as workable as concentrated times. In general, these studies have disclosed that people show severe interference when even very simple tasks are performed at the same time, if both tasks require selecting and producing action*

(e.g., (Gladstones, Regan & Lee 1989) (Pashler 1994)). Many researchers believe that action planning represents a "bottleneck", which the human brain can only perform one task at a time. Psychiatrist Edward M. Hallowell has gone so far as to describe multitasking as a "mythical activity in which people believe they can perform two or more tasks simultaneously as effectively as one. [2]

The *Wikipedia* article even points out that some researchers believe it is impossible to learn new information while multitasking. To multitask is literally to handicap yourself. Humans simply don't do more than one thing at the same time, no matter what your resume says.

And when you really come to think about it, this becomes rather obvious (as long as you are not thinking about something else at the same time, of course). Taking one task on with your full attention allows you to, well; take on that task with your full attention. And thus, you can defeat whatever foe lies before you by putting your all into it. Otherwise, even rather simple tasks can pile up on top of each other and become a disorienting blob of confusion that leads first to frustration, then to working on something else, them coming back to the original project, trying to reorient yourself, feeling overwhelmed and finally, giving in to procrastination.

Single-tasking is, unfortunately, not as easy to do as to explain. There's not just some switch to flip. This is especially true for managers who have subordinates asking questions

2. "Human multitasking", Wikipedia.org, http://en.wikipedia.org/wiki/Human_multitasking, Accessed 4/12/2015

of them at all times about a variety of different subjects or for those in customer service being barraged by various customers. Still, whenever possible, it's best to focus on one thing and one thing only. And when going back and forth between things is unavoidable, it's best to find ways to mitigate this problem as much as possible.

Here are some handy methods I've used to do this:

- **Scheduling Distractions**: Schedule times to deal with such issues and make sure everyone knows that unless it's an emergency, save your questions for that time.
- **Avoid Distractions**: Try to have a relatively quiet work area.
- **Lists**: Utilize to do lists (or Getting Things Done® to be discussed in Chapter 5)
- **Remove Clutter**: Keep your computer, work area and desk clean (cluttered desk equals cluttered mind).
- **Change Completely**: If you must divert your attention to a new matter, put the old task to bed for a while before returning to it.

But whatever you do, don't settle for the easy way out, which is mindless multitasking. All kidding aside, what I would like to see on those resumes is something like "Can avoid the temptation of multitasking and focus on a single task at a time until it is complete."

3

Speed Reading

Speed reading may very well be the best thing since sliced bread. Or for paleo enthusiasts such as myself, sliced meat, I guess. In my own experience, I have at least doubled and possibly tripled my reading speed allowing me to plow through books at a rate I could not have imagined before. Indeed, I read more than twice as many books in 2014 than I did in 2013.

The process is rather simple, although it is a bit awkward at first and takes a little time to get used to. Luckily there are only two major points:

1. Use a pen or similar object to track along each line: This keeps your eyes moving along with the pen and prevents them from backtracking instead of moving in a consistent linear motion. As H. Bernard Wechsler notes in *Speed Reading for Professionals*, "Studies have demonstrated that college graduates tend to backtrack about twenty times per page." [1]

2. Don't pronounce the words in your mind: We all naturally pronounce the words we read in our heads in what's called subvocalization. However, we all have the ability to recognize words without subvocalization and can do so much quicker than we can pronounce them. So if you learn to read using simple recognition, you can drastically increase your speed.

1. H. Bernard Wechsler and Arthur Bell, *Speed Reading for Professionals*, Barron's Business Success Series, January 1, 2006, Pg. 29

Some other tips I've heard include using your peripheral vision to read the edges of the page to limit the distance your eyes have to move and even learning to lump certain common phrases together. For example, Tim Ferriss makes the case that,

> *You must use conditioning drills to increase horizontal peripheral vision span and the number of words registered per fixation. Untrained subjects use central focus but not horizontal peripheral vision span during reading, foregoing up to 50% of their words per fixation (the number of words that can be perceived and "read" in each fixation).* [2]

I don't use these methods, and I certainly haven't found them necessary. Although, I do believe they could aid in helping me read even faster. That being said, I've been able to speed read without reducing my comprehension, but when I've tried to add this element, it's been harder to retain what I've read. And of course, what's the point of reading in the first place if you're not going to remember anything? That would be like high school all over again.

When starting out, I would read two to four pages with speed reading and then take two pages off and just read them normally. This way, I didn't wear myself out or lose interest in the project entirely as it's not easy when starting. As time went

2. Tim Ferriss, "Scientific Speed Reading: How to Read 300% Faster in 20 Minutes", *The Blog of Tim Ferris*, http://fourhourworkweek.com/2009/07/30/speed-reading-and-accelerated-learning/, July 30, 2009

on it became more and more natural and I had to take fewer and fewer "breaks."

That being said, I don't always speed read and you should feel no need to always do it. I don't hold a pen up to my computer monitor when reading an email. And if I'm just relaxing on the beach with some book, I don't usually feel the need to speed read. It's not a "have to" type of thing, but it certainly comes in handy. Remember, reading should be enjoyable.

If you are interesting in learning this technique, I would definitely recommend Tim Ferriss' article and practice methods in his article "Scientific Speed Reading" on his website FourHourWorkWeek.com.

4

Getting Things Done®

The human mind is great at coming up with ideas, but terrible at storing them.

This is the key insight that the great organizational expert David Allen realized many years ago. As he noted,

> *A basic truism I have discovered over twenty years of coaching and training is that most of the stress people experience comes from inappropriately managed commitments they make or accept.* [1]

As noted in the chapter on multitasking, people are barraged with various things to do or keep track of. We have fooled ourselves into thinking that the best way to manage this situation is to learn how to be superheroes and do the impossible by doing all sorts of things at the same time while also remembering all sorts of commitments and critical information sandwiched in between useless trivia about the Kardashians or whatever.

And of course, as mentioned before, this is folly. And it's not just folly in my experience or by some pop-psychology nonsense you'll hear on Oprah. David Allen does even science, dude. The eminent psychologist George Miller explained the

1. David Allen, *Getting Things Done*, Penguin Books, December 31, 2002, Pg. 12

limits of human memory in his extremely influential paper on the subject,

> *Everybody knows that there is a finite span of immediate memory and that for a lot of different kinds of test materials this span is about seven items in length. I have just shown you that there is a span of absolute judgment that can distinguish about seven categories and that there is a span of attention that will encompass about six objects at a glance.* [2]

Over and over again throughout the paper, Miller finds that the number of things a person can keep at the top of their mind at the same time is about seven, plus or minus two. This has come to be known as Miller's Law and is a finding that has been repeatedly validated (in fact, many scientists now think it's actually more like four). [3]

So what do we do when we're confronted with so many disparate tasks and pieces of information that we can barely sort, let alone remember? Well we almost certainly put too much or too little (or none at all) emphasis on them. Instead, in an ideal world, we should react to various stimuli with a "mind like water." As David Allen puts it,

> *Imagine throwing a pebble in a pond. How does the water respond? The answer is, totally appropriately to*

2. George A. Miller, *The Magical Number Seven*, Plus or Minus Two: Some Limits on our Capacity for Processing Information, Psychological Review, 63, Pg. 81-97, 1956
3. See for example, Clara Moskowitz, *Mind's Limit Found: 4 Things at Once*, Live Science, http://www.livescience.com/2493-mind-limit-4.html, April 27, 2008

the force and mass of the input; then it returns to calm. It doesn't overreact or underreact. [4]

And when you have a firm grasp of all of your commitments, it makes it so much easier to react appropriately to any given input. Indeed, my computer and desk (both the one at the office and at home) were awash in to do lists and notes prior to using David Allen's method called GTD (Getting Things Done®). And I was consistently stressed out. Afterwards, I don't stress at all about remembering what I need to do, it's all in my "trusted system."

To explain the whole system would take too long (and probably break copyright law), but in brief, you filter all of your "inputs" such as emails, letters, things to do, etc. into different categories. If it's something you can do in two minutes, you just do it. If it's something you need to do, you put it under "action items," if it's something you're waiting for, you put it under "waiting for," and if it's something you want to discuss with someone, you put it under "agenda item." Finally, if it requires two or more steps, you put it under "projects" along with the next action step to accomplish said project.

There's of course a lot more to it than that, but GTD creates a system whereby everything you need to do is right there in front of you and out of your mind. Another key advantage is that the system is extremely flexible and can be adapted to paper systems or online systems. In many ways, I would describe it as more of framework than anything else. It's a framework designed to get those thoughts out of your head

---

4. David Allen, *Getting Things Done*, Penguin Books, December 31, 2002, Pg. 11

and into a trusted system. For example, my brother uses GTD with a bunch of notepads he carries around in a binder while I use the online program Evernote.

And indeed, along with a ton of anecdotal data, there is scientific evidence that implies GTD works. When Roy Baumeister and John Tierney studied what increased willpower, David Allen's method kept coming up. They discuss the Zeigarnik Effect that saps mental energy when tasks are left incomplete. Basically, our mind wants to wrap these projects up and close the loop. When we don't, mental energy is used just remembering said task. Open loops sap your willpower.

But if you can remove those tasks from your mind and put them in your trusted system, you can save that mental energy. Baumeister and Tierney conclude that "...there is evidence in the psychological literature of the mental stress that Allen observed" and also mention one powerful anecdote,

> ...when the technology writer Danny O'Brien sent a questionnaire asking seventy of the most "sickeningly prolific" people he knew for their organization secrets, most said they didn't use special software or other elaborate tools. But a good many did say they followed the GTD system... [5]

I suspect the reason for this is not just that GTD increased productivity, but also that GTD keeps important, but not highly visible items on your radar. These are the issues that

5. Roy Baumeister and John Tierney, *Willpower*, Penguin Books, August 28, 2012, Pg. 80

Stephen Covey refers to as being in Quadrant 2, or things that are important, but not urgent. This not only prevents problems from becoming crises by dealing with them ahead of time, but also opens up all sorts of opportunities that would otherwise have slid by under the radar. I'll let Stephen Covey explain why Quadrant 2 thinking is so important,

> *[Quadrant 2] deals with things like building relationships, writing a personal mission statement, long-range planning, exercising, preventive maintenance, preparation—all those things we know we need to do, but somehow seldom get around to doing, because they aren't urgent. To paraphrase Peter Drucker, effective people are not problem-minded; they're opportunity-minded. They feed opportunities and starve problems. They think preventively.* [6]

To do lists are full of Quadrant 1 items (urgent and important) or easy stuff that isn't important at all. To do lists are full of whatever thing is the loudest and the squeaky wheel tends to get the grease. But that's not how it necessarily should be. Malcom Gladwell references "The 10,000-Hour Rule"[7] in his famous book *Outliers* that states that for someone to master something, it takes about 10,000 hours of practice. And while that statistic has been criticized,[8] it is obviously true that to

---

6. Stephen Covey, *The 7 Habits of Highly Effective People*, Simon and Schuster Inc., Copyright 1987, Pg, 153-154
7. Malcolm Gladwell, *Outliers*, Hachette Book Group, Inc., Copyright 2008, Pg. 35
8. See for example Daniel Goleman, "Why the 10,000 Hour Rule Is A Myth," *The Huff-*

become great at something, it requires a lot of sustained effort. And it's not always effort toward something urgent.

GTD will not automatically point you toward Quadrant 2, but it does create a framework that is perfectly designed to manage your life in a way that brings Quadrant 2 activities to the forefront. In my judgment, it is definitely worth giving a try.

You can learn more about GTD at David Allen's website *GettingThingsDone.com* or in his book *Getting Things Done.* [9]

ington Post, http://www.huffingtonpost.com/2013/10/08/success-book_n_4059506.html, October 10th, 2013
9. Author's note: Neither I nor Thought Catalog is affiliated with David Allen or his organization in any way.

5

Pareto's Autopilot

One of the best ways to accomplish more is to get stuff done without even doing it. Or at the very least you could cut down the number of steps involved in doing each given task.

There's something called Pareto's Principle, or the 80/20 principle. It's named after the nineteenth century economist Vilfredo Pareto who determined that 80 percent of the wealth in Italy was owned by 20 percent of the people. He then found this same ratio applied itself in many other places and to many other things. As the *Wikipedia* article on the subject notes, claims have been made that,

> *80% of a company's profits come from 20% of its customers...80% of a company's sales come from 20% of its products...20% of patients have been found to use 80% of health care resources. Several criminology studies have found that 80% of crimes are committed by 20% of criminals.* [1]

And so on.

The important thing for this discussion, however, is the principle that 80 percent of your results come from 20 percent

1. "Pareto principle", Wikipedia.org, http://en.wikipedia.org/wiki/Pareto_principle, Accessed April 19, 2015

of your actions. In all likelihood, that can be split again and 64 percent of your results come from 4 percent of your actions.

So obviously the key is to expand the amount of time you spend on that 20 percent. Or better yet, on that 4 percent.

Indeed, it is rather sickening to think about how much of what we do is tedious, repetitive and could be done by just about anyone else (or anything else). If we feel we are worth, say, $25 an hour, why would we spend time doing a task worthy of a job worth only $10 an hour?

And when it comes to our personal life, why would do some of these things at all?

Productivity expert Ari Meisel actually put pen to pad to figure out how many steps there are in a variety of various, mundane activities. Take paying a bill for example. As he put it,

> The average number of steps required to pay a bill is 27… That may sound crazy… If I asked you right now, 'how do you pay a bill?' you would probably just tell me 'oh well, I just go to the bank website and pay it and that's it.' And you have like three things that you do, but the truth is it's more than that. You go to the banking website, you login, you go to the payee website, is the payee already there? If they are not, you have to add them. And this is the process for adding them. This is the account you like to use, this is the date you like to send them. So on and so forth and it very quickly get to 27 steps. [2]

2. Ari Meisel, "My Productivity Secret", *The Tom Woods Podcast*, http://tomwoods.com/podcast/ep-376-my-productivity-secret/, April 8, 2015

He recommends that you "optimize, automate and outsource" everything you can do so there's "less doing and more living" in your life. Start with optimizing. A simple example could be making a checklist for a routine, but rather long activity. That way you can just blast through it without spending any time thinking about the steps necessary. (And maybe keep all of these checklists in your GTD system.) Or if you have a group of colleagues or friends you email often, make that a set group in your email account so you don't have to individually add them each time. It may take just a few seconds to do so, but as this process repeats itself over and over again, those seconds add up.

Personally, I have to email a bunch of financial information to banks all the time for loan applications for our business. So instead of attaching each document (there's about 30 of them) to each set of emails, I just have the emails under a Gmail label and forward them to whatever bank as it comes up.

There are countless things like this that you can do that can shave seconds here or minutes there and give you more time to either be even more productive or just live your life.

One of the best ways to determine this is to actually track what you do for an entire week. Create a spreadsheet broken out by either every 15 or 30 minutes and then write down every task you did during the week. Then review this spreadsheet and ask yourself which of these tasks you can optimize. Then ask which you can automate. And then ask whether you need to do them at all. Meisel again,

> *Most of these activities are routine. We can do*
> *them without even thinking, almost as if on*

autopilot. While this might seem like a good thing, the truth is if you can get these things done on autopilot, someone else could, too. [3]

So for certain tasks, you could delegate them to a coworker or subordinate, or you could find a virtual assistant on Elance or Odesk to help you with some of these tasks. For example, I have a lot of data entry that I have a virtual assistant in the Philippines do for three dollars an hour. Maybe you feel guilty about paying so little, but the median monthly salary in the Philippines is only about $630 a week. [4] The cost of living is much less in the Philippines than the United States, and while there is unfortunately a lot to of poverty there as well, three dollars an hour is right in line with and probably higher than the median income. Poor countries don't become rich overnight, so all you're doing is offering a job that would make someone better off than they were before. And in this case, it doesn't make financial sense for our company to offer someone in the United States $10/hour to do this. I would just have to do it myself (or do without it entirely), so it makes me more productive and provides a job to someone who needs it. In other words, it is really just a net benefit.

Either way, tracking the various things you do and then either optimizing, automating or outsourcing as much of that as possible can make you all the more productive and give you all the more time to simply live your life. So get on it!

3. Ari Meisel, *Less Doing, More Living*, Jeremy P. Tarcher/Penguin, April 3, 2014, Pg. 8
4. Salary Explorer, "Salary Survey in Philippines", http://www.salaryexplorer.com/salary-survey.php?loc=171&loctype=1, Accessed April 19, 2015. Based on currency conversion as of April 19, 2015.

Part 2

Conquering Fear

6

Contextualize and Embrace Your Fear

Fear is one of, if not the greatest, barriers to success and happiness that we all face. It keeps people, myself included, mired in stagnation and mediocrity. Thereby, conquering fear is of critical importance.

The first thing to note is that fear is often useful. It is not something that we should try to defeat per se, it's something that we need to understand and overcome. Fear evolved to protect us from that hungry saber tooth tiger or whatever other danger lied behind the bushes. Today however, in our advanced and much safer world, it tends to be counterproductive and even debilitating. But it's not fear itself that is counterproductive; it is caving to that fear.

Understanding that everyone deals with fear about a whole range of things is the first important insight. No one is alone when it comes to fear. But recognizing that "Most men lead lives of quiet desperation and go to the grave with the song still in them" as Henry David Thoreau has been misquoted as saying[1] does not bind us to the same fate. In fact, recognizing fear's universality is the first step to liberating us from it.

1. Henry David Thoreau Mis-Quotation Page", The Walden Project, https://www.walden.org/Library/Quotations/The_Henry_D._Thoreau_Mis-Quotation_Page, Accessed April 20th, 2015

Virtually every time that I can remember a famous or successful person opening up, they discuss the many fears they had along the way. For example, Warren Buffet admitted he was "terrified" [2] of public speaking and Lebron James admitted to having a severe "fear of failure." [3]

In addition to recognizing that fear is universal to humanity, it is also important to identify what particular issue is causing said fear. Most fears boil down to either a fear of the unknown or a fear of criticism. Isolating the causes of fear can by itself help dispel them because many, once stated explicitly, become visibly absurd.

So figure out what the fear actually is and then list out what the potential consequences could be. Are you afraid of asking that girl/guy out? OK, well the fear is probably of 1) not knowing how he/she will respond (fear of the unknown) and 2) being rejected (fear of criticism). But so what if you are rejected? Has your state of being—not being in a relationship with said person—changed at all?

Dale Carnegie gave one such anecdote in his famous book *How to Stop Worrying and Start Living*, noting that,

> *After discovering the worst that could possibly happen and reconciling myself to accepting it, if necessary, an extremely important thing hap-*

2. Carmine Gallo, "How Warren Buffett and Joel Osteen Conquered Their Terrifying Fear of Public Speaking", *Forbes*, http://www.forbes.com/sites/carminegallo/2013/05/16/how-warren-buffett-and-joel-osteen-conquered-their-terrifying-fear-of-public-speaking/, May 16, 2013

3. Matt Moore, "Lebron James: 'I'm afraid of failure'", *CBS Sports*, http://www.cbssports.com/nba/eye-on-basketball/24087923/lebron-james-im-afraid-of-failure, October 15, 2013

pened: I immediately relaxed and felt a sense of
peace that I hadn't experienced in days. [4]

And that's after accepting the worst that could happen! Indeed, my father once told me that 99 percent of the things we worry about don't end up coming true at all. That may not be technically accurate, but it sounds about right given my experience worrying about all sorts of irrelevant fantasies and fictions.

And even for those fears that do come to pass, they are usually not nearly as bad as they originally seem. From my experience at least, it is usually the unexpected things that blindside us which cause most of life's problems, not the things we are incessantly worrying about.

Most people (myself included) get too wrapped up in the minutia of everyday life that we forget to look at the bigger picture. We become attached to and mentally exhausted by all of this baggage. Brian Tracey, in his excellent book *Change Your Thinking, Change Your Life,* mentions that,

> *The great spiritual teachers, such as Buddha and*
> *Jesus, have emphasized the importance of separat-*
> *ing yourself emotionally from the situation*
> *(disidentification), in order to regain your calm-*
> *ness and composure.* [5]

4. Dale Carnegie, *How to Stop Worrying and Start Living*, Pocket Books, September 15, 1990, Pg. 14
5. Brian Tracey, Change Your Thinking, Change Your Life, John Wiley and Sons, Inc., August 15th, Pg. 24

Separating ourselves from the situation and even the potential outcomes can be of great service when it comes to fear. Just compare whatever problem you're facing to the size and history of the universe and it starts to seem rather trivial.

Even our own mortality can be viewed in a way to alleviate fear. As one popular Youtuber noted "we all die" and that once we accept this, all we need to ask is "Will this thing you're afraid of matter in 300 years?" [6] Once you really start to think about it, in all likelihood, it probably won't even matter next week.

OK, but we're all irrational and not being aware of that irrationality is in itself irrational. Recognizing that a fear is ridiculous doesn't make it go away, even if it does diminish the effects of it.

But we shouldn't want fear to go away. Instead, we should go even further and actually embrace our fear. As Susan Jeffers notes in her fantastic book *Feel the Fear and Do It Anyways*, "The fear will never go away as long as [you] continue to grow." [7] This is because, as mentioned above, one of the greatest fears is that of the unknown. And thereby, whenever you're doing something new or reaching a new level in your career, life or relationships, it will be scary.

And it should be.

Fear is thereby often a good thing; a sign that you are growing or taking on something new. If you ever think to yourself, "you know, I haven't been afraid of something for a long time," it probably means you are doing something wrong.

6. Storm Clouds Gathering, "How to Overcome Fear When Facing Real Danger", https://www.youtube.com/watch?v=9pnqWGBYP7Q, October 8th, 2014
7. Susan Jeffers, *Feel the Fear... and Do It Anyway*, Random House Publishing Group Copyright 1987, Pg. 22

So embrace fear and seek after that which makes you afraid.

7

Honesty

Robert Glover asked a very interesting question that I think is worth pondering,

> *Why would it seem rational for a person to try to eliminate or hide certain things about himself and try to become something different unless there was a compelling reason for him to do so? Why do people try to change who they are?* [1]

OK, we should all try to change and improve. The provocative point here is about hiding something about ourselves. Why hide something unless we are ashamed of it? Why hide something unless we are afraid of being found out?

One of the biggest, most consistent fears is the fear of being judged, criticized or ridiculed. I would say it's almost universal in our society. This fear makes us seek out after mediocrity as 1) any sort of risk can lead to failure which can be ridiculed and 2) success or mere uniqueness breeds attention, which can lead to criticism. Indeed, many of us are afraid of being successful. Think about it; try to name even one famous person who isn't being criticized nearly all of the time.

1. Robert Glover, *No More Mr. Nice Guy*, Barnes and Noble Publishing Inc., Copyright 2003, Pg. 19

Accepting that criticism is universal is the first step to overcome this fear, but being honest is also of the utmost importance. Living a life in the shadows creates a sort of paranoia; "what if I get found out?" Furthermore, as Glover noted above, hiding something means you are almost certainly ashamed of it, even if there is no reason to be.

I remember one time I was embarrassed about breaking a chair at a friend's house. There were multiple people there but no witnesses to this terrible negligence, so I probably could have just swept it under the rug. One of the other guests could have taken the fall. Or it might be left as one of history's great mysteries. But instead, I mustered up the modicum of courage necessary to admit my grave misdeed. "Meh, whatever" was the response.

Indeed, if people already know whatever it is you are afraid of them finding out, well, then there's quite obviously nothing to be found out. And thereby, there's nothing to fear. If you made some mistake, admit it quickly and fully. Generally, people can't even be bothered to care.

This is not always the case, of course. Sometimes there are consequences. But generally speaking, it is better to accept them (and learn from them) then to live in fear of being discovered. Hiding from others makes it easier to hide from ourselves. And then we just keep repeating the same mistakes over and over again. Most transgressions can be forgiven. And people will generally appreciate the honesty and thereby quicken the process of getting past whatever issue is in question. Indeed, in all likelihood, they'll figure out whatever you are hiding one way or another.

And if nothing else, research shows that being honest improves your health. [2]

Now obviously there is a point at which such honesty becomes excessive. Nobody wants to hear your full life story; most of it is probably as boring as mine and some of it is kind of gross. But, these aren't really the things we're afraid to tell (or would feel any compunction to tell in the first place). It's our flaws and mistakes that we are afraid of. But all these flaws and mistakes do is signal to other people that we're just as human as they are. It's hard to empathize with someone who's flawless and even harder with someone who merely pretends to be.

In fact, I would once again go even further. Demand that your friends, family, supervisors, colleagues and subordinates give you honest feedback and give it to them as well. Don't merely accept polite platitudes that allow us to maintain a comfortable and oblivious mediocrity.

Live out loud and the fear will be drowned out by the noise.

2. Lying Less Linked to Better Health, New Research Finds", American Psychological Association, http://www.apa.org/news/press/releases/2012/08/lying-less.aspx, August 4th, 2012

8

Lean Just Outside Your Comfort Zone

The only sure way to get rid of the fear of doing something is to go out and do it. – Susan Jeffers [1]

She is absolutely right. We can all think of things that were terrifying when we first did them but now don't give us a second thought. I remember be scared to death the first time I jumped off the high dive. Now I couldn't care less. I was so frightened of the "big" rollercoasters when I was a kid that I would stick to the Ferris wheel (and still be nervous about that, too). Today I love rollercoasters.

That being said, taking on what can seem like the whole world all at once is an overwhelming task sure to crush someone's courage in a heartbeat. The key to defeating fear and building courage is to simply take one step at a time.

So, if you have a fear of public speaking, don't try to give a massive presentation to a packed audience right out of the gate. The fear will almost certainly paralyze you and defeat the whole project before it even begins. Instead, join Toastmasters or something to that effect. Then once you have become

1. Susan Jeffers, *Feel the Fear... and Do It Anyway,* Ballantine Books, December 26, 2006, Pg. 23

comfortable with that, you can take the next step. So on and so forth.

A famous saying goes that "comfort makes cowards of us all." So don't let yourself get comfortable! As noted before, you must come to embrace fear. It is your ally, not your enemy, if you treat it as such. Try to constantly stay just outside of your comfort zone. Live in that state. Embrace that state. Demand that state. That way you are always pushing yourself further ahead without the risk of becoming overwhelmed.

One way to help maintain that state is to put your courage on autopilot. Research has shown that the simple act of making decisions can be exhausting. [2] Sometimes you just need to give yourself simple rules to follow in certain situations. For example, one of the best proposed rules I've heard and started to use was from Brian Tracey,

> *There is a rule that I have learned from experience: Never do or refrain from doing something because you are concerned about what people might think about you. The fact is that nobody is even thinking about you at all.* [3]

Afraid to send an email to an old friend for no other reason than to catch up? Why? Are you afraid she might judge you? Not good enough. Sent.

Rules like this should be automatic and can defeat fears before they even come up. Of course, we have to remember

2. See for example "Decision Fatigue", Wikipedia, http://en.wikipedia.org/wiki/Decision_fatigue, Accessed April 20th, 2015
3. Brian Tracey, *Change Your Thinking, Change Your Life*, John Wiley and Sons, Inc., August 15th, Pg. 26

that practice makes perfect (although, as already mentioned, fear never goes away nor should you want it to). Along the way, mistakes are to be expected. In fact, like fear, mistakes are often signs that we are growing and trying new things (see Chapter 11). They should be embraced as well.

If you are ready for some advanced, fear-crushing exercises, check out the challenges Timothy Ferris gives in his book *The Four Hour Work Week*. [4] Or make up some challenges for yourself, such as starting a conversation with a stranger on the bus or traveling abroad.

Just don't stop leaning.

---

4. See Timothy Ferris, *The 4-Hour Workweek*, Random House, Inc., Copyright 2009 or for a list of the exercises, see "Comfort Challenges", *High Existence*, Accessed April 20th, 2015, http://www.highexistence.com/topic/comfort-challenges/

Part 3

Wellness

9

Minimalism

Much of the modern world seems to be a conspiracy set against us to make us believe that we live the most boring existence this world has ever known. Not only does the media bombard us with images, stories and videos of awesome people (fictional or nonfictional) doing awesome things, but we have the new social media to let us know that even the people in our social network are doing awesome things too.

Someone just got married and posted several thousand pictures from their wedding and reception. Another just traveled to some exotic foreign land. Parties and festivities were had. Jane has a new boyfriend. John got a promotion. Facebook statuses have assured us that Alex and Lisa are simply elated with how great life is. And good lord, it appears every woman I've ever met that has had a baby has posted about 10,000 pictures of said child.

This all represents "FoMo" or the Fear of Missing Out. As *Wikipedia* describes it, FoMo is the "pervasive apprehension that others might be having rewarding experiences from which one is absent." [1] Of course, it's mostly an illusion, the posts showing up in your feed will be disproportionately from those who just did something cool. When you actually aver-

---

1. Fear of Missing Out", Wikipedia, Accessed April 25, 2015, http://en.wikipedia.org/wiki/Fear_of_missing_out

age it out against everyone, that person is probably just as boring as you.

And of course this goes for stuff as well. The desire to keep up with the Jones' or show how awesome you are by buying more stuff is about as shallow as it seems. Yet studies have found that the amount of income you have has almost no effect on your level of happiness. [2] But that hasn't stopped Americans from trying to buy it. For example, the average U.S. household had over $15,000 in credit card debt in 2014. [3]

But maybe you say that that's just stuff. FoMO has more to do with experiences. True, but they are both based on the same thing; the idea that the grass is greener on the other side of fence. The fear that someone has something cooler than you, a better job, a hotter spouse, more exciting experiences, more useful skills, whatever.

Indeed, all Facebook and Twitter do is mask others' struggles and allow you to see only the best foot forward that hundreds of friends have to put forth. A Stanford study showed that exact thing,

> *For all four experiences (feeling really depressed for a day, feeling very lonely on a weekend night, being sad enough about something in their lives that they cried, and feeling overwhelmed by schoolwork or extracurricular activities), students at both universities underestimated peer preva-*

2. See for example Eric Quiñones, "Link between income and happiness is mainly an illusion", News at Princeton, June 29, 2006, http://www.princeton.edu/main/news/archive/S15/15/09S18/index.xml?section=topstories
3. Tim Chen, "American Household Credit Card Debt Statistics: 2014", *Nerd Wallet*, Accessed April 25, 2015, http://www.nerdwallet.com/blog/credit-card-data/average-credit-card-debt-household/

lence… At one university, students estimated that 52% of their peers had felt depressed, 38% had felt lonely, 43% had cried, and 78% had felt over-whelmed by work, whereas respectively 78%, 56%, 66%, and 94% of students reported having actu-ally had each of these four experiences. [4]

Another study found that Facebook (and probably all social media) actually made this all the worse.

These analyses indicated that Facebook use pre-dicts declines in the two components of subjective well-being: how people feel moment to moment and how satisfied they are with their lives. [5]

And yet Americans spend an average of 40 minutes a day on Facebook [6] and that doesn't include Twitter and other social networks. Indeed, a British think tank called Penisula even estimated that Facebook costs Britain 2.8 billion hours of worker productivity annually. [7] And I wonder how much time spent in full on FoMO while starring at one's Facebook feed

4. Alexander H. Jordan, Benoit Monin, Carol S. Dweck, Benjamin J. Lovett, Oliver P. John and James J. Gross, "Misery Has Mor Company Than People Think," Personality and Social Psychology Bulletin 37, Copyright 2011, Pg. 123

5. Ethan Kross, Philippe Verduyun, Emre Demiralp, Jiyoung Park, David Seungjae Lee, Natalie Lin, Holly Shablack, John Jonides, Oscar Vbarra, "Facebook Use Predicts Declines in Subjective Well-Being in Young Adults", PLOS One, August 14, 2013, http://journals.plos.org/plosone/article?id=10.1371/journal.pone.0069841#s3

6. Joshua Brustein, "Americans Now Spend More Time on Facebook Than They Do on Their Pets", Bloomberg, July 23, 2014, http://www.bloomberg.com/bw/articles/2014-07-23/heres-how-much-time-people-spend-on-facebook-daily

7. Facebook 'costs business dear'", BBC News, September 11, 2007, http://news.bbc.co.uk/2/hi/technology/6989100.stm

could have been spent doing something productive or fun for that matter.

The same could go for television, which too much exposure to has been associated with depression.[8] Yet a report from Bureau of Labor Statistics finds that the average American watches almost three hours of TV per day.[9] That represents close to 20 percent of their waking lives!

Despite the message we get from those televisions we watch too much of, the world has improved greatly in recent decades,[10] yet this has created a subsidiary problem, namely an overabundance of stuff and choices. Merely surviving is not enough. In the past, merely surviving and helping those you cared about survive could provide purpose. Nowadays, finding purpose is much more difficult.

My case is that you will not find purpose in stuff nor will you in media of the old fashioned or 2.0 variety. These things will just make you spin faster and faster on the wheel in the rat race and make you feel more and more like you are missing out.

Indeed, I have no interest in returning to the days of medieval peasants who constantly faced starvation or 19th-century factory workers who would put in 60-80 hours a week in grueling conditions. But we can choose to simplify our own lives. Instead of worrying about who's doing something that

8. Jessica Firger, "Depression, loneliness linked to binge-watching TV", *CBS News*, January 29, 2015, http://www.cbsnews.com/news/depression-loneliness-linked-to-binge-watching-television/

9. American Time Use Survey Summary", Bureau of Labor Statistics, June 18, 2014, http://www.bls.gov/news.release/atus.nr0.htm

10. See for example, "Human Progress", http://humanprogress.org/, Accessed May 17, 2014

we're not invited too, or drowning ourselves in stuff or media, we can try to focus on a few attainable goals and relationships.

First and foremost, I would stop worrying about stuff entirely. If you want to make your house look nice, fine, go for it. And go ahead and buy nice clothes. Looking sharp is important. But otherwise, it should be merely functional. If you don't need X toy or Y electronic, don't buy it. And ladies, four or five pairs of shoes should be sufficient.

I've lived life without a TV for the last five years and I couldn't speak higher of it. Yes, I binge watched *Breaking Bad* on my computer, but I haven't channel surfed once in the last five years. I've limited my media consumption to only the things I absolutely want to see the most.

Only of late have I tried to limit my Internet media consumption and it's much more difficult. But I can see already how important it is. Everything we do means we can't do something else. In economics, this is called an opportunity cost. And yes, while the Internet is great, much of it is junk that just means you couldn't have done something more productive or fun.

Minimalism in both stuff and media won't eliminate choice paralysis or FoMO, but it will help a lot. You can't do everything! So try to cut out the fat. Prioritize what are the most important things in your life and who are the most important people in your life and try to focus on those. Get rid of the extraneous stuff. Learn to be OK with letting some fad pass you by without trying it. Remember the 10,000 hour rule Gladwell discussed? You aren't going to be great at anything if you keep starting and stopping. If the average American watches 3 hours of TV a week, that amounts to 76,440 hours of television between the time they are born and the time they reach the age of 70. In that time, you could have mastered seven different skills and be halfway to the eighth instead!

If you don't like something, sure, stop it. But don't give up on X if you like it just because Y came by and looks cooler now. In all likelihood it won't look cooler in a month.

And as far as stuff goes, just go by a local garage sale and ask yourself how much of that stuff the seller actually needed when he or she bought it. Probably not very much.

Cut out the clutter, unplug the TV, reduce your time on social media and focus on what is of primary importance to you. In other words, embrace minimalism.

10

Embracing Mistakes

Just like with fear, pretty much without exception, every successful individual I've heard speak has recounted the many mistakes they've made before becoming successful. These anti-nostalgic trips down memory lane do make one feel better about their own mistakes and perhaps help one to realize such blunders are just part of the learning curve. Indeed, the list of failures by successful people is quite long. For example,

- Bill Gates' first business failed miserably
- Richard Branson did terrible in school
- The Beatles were rejected by Decca Records
- Dr. Seuss' first book was rejected 27 times
- Stephen King's first novel was rejected 30 times
- Emily Dickinson published fewer than a dozen of her 1,800 poems during her lifetime [1]

However, it is not uncommon for there to be an unstated yet harmful undercurrent to these discussions. They often come with a vibe that screwing up was a problem in the past and only in the past. Something like, "Yes, before I became suc-

---

1. Examples taken from Renee Jacques, "16 Wildly Successful People Who Overcame Huge Obstacles To Get There", *The Huffington Post*, http://www.huffingtonpost.com/2013/09/25/successful-people-obstacles_n_3964459.html, February 13, 2014

cessful, I made a lot of mistakes. Then I became successful and voilà!"

The secret that is often left unstated is that no one stops making mistakes. There is no point when someone becomes "successful" and stops screwing up. Life doesn't work like that.

Jeff Bewkes was the CEO of Time Warner when he orchestrated the disastrous merger with AOL (at the time, AOL was valued at $226 billion, by 2015, it was valued at $20 billion).[2] Presumably Bewkes was successful when he made that decision. And George Lucas followed up the original *Star Wars* films with the Jar Jar Binks and an eight year old Darth Vader yelling "Yipppeee!"

Life is about climbing higher through a series of inevitable mistakes. Or as Michael Jordan put it in what is indisputably the greatest sports commercial of all time,

> *I've missed more than 9,000 shots in my career.*
> *I've lost almost 300 games. Twenty-six times, I've*
> *been trusted to take the game winning shot and*
> *missed. I've failed over and over and over again in*
> *my life. And that is why I succeed.*[3]

Failure, like fear, is something to be embraced, not avoided. My brother keeps a sign in his office reading "Make More Mistakes" and lucky for me, I haven't had much difficulty following through with this advice.

2. Rita Gunther McGrath, "15 years later, lessons from the failed AOL-Time Warner merger", *Forbes*, http://fortune.com/2015/01/10/15-years-later-lessons-from-the-failed-aol-time-warner-merger/, January 10, 2015
3. Michael Jordan "Failure" Nike Commercial", Nike, Viewable at https://www.youtube.com/watch?v=45mMioJ5szc, Accessed May 2, 2015

I'm a real estate investor by trade. On more than one occasion I bought a house with a broken sewer line, unbeknownst to me. Once you flush $3500 down the drain enough times, you eventually learn your lesson. So we started scoping the sewer lines before purchasing older homes and it has been well worth it.

Thus, in the long run, this was a good thing, not a bad one. I learned a lesson from it and became better at my job. Mistakes aren't just part of the learning curve, they are part of life. While errors are more common when getting your footing in a new field, experience can lead to its own unique set of mistakes, such as overconfidence and apathy. Yet the fear that many people have of screwing up can be the biggest hindrance to jumping in and moving forward. Well, for those who are afraid of such things, let me assure you that you will make plenty of mistakes.

Accept it and embrace it.

Indeed, many mistakes are actually a sign of progress. They show we are trying something new or pushing ahead. Of course, that doesn't mean to be reckless. But sooner rather than later we need to jump in to whatever it is we are aiming to do. You will then inevitably screw up and then learn, improve and move on.

As former IBM CEO Thomas Watson said, "The fastest way to succeed is to double your rate of failure." Summer Redstone was even more blunt, "Great success is built on failure, frustration, even catastrophe." [4] And we all know what

---

4. "But They Did Not Give Up", University of Kentucky, http://www.uky.edu/~eushe2/Pajares/OnFailingG.html, Accessed May 2, 2015

Thomas Edison had to say about his first 1,000 attempts at the incandescent light bulb.

Embrace that you will make mistakes in the future and forgive yourself for those in the past. As the Chinese proverb says, "every day is a new life to the wise man." Just make sure you've learned the lessons from your previous lives as you proceed with the next one.

11

The Early Bird

As the saying goes, the early bird gets the worm. Personally, I've never been an early riser. I like late nights and even more so, I like late mornings. I like sleep. That being said, waking up early can be a huge benefit.

It's not easy, for sure. I hate it. Steve Pavlina recommends practicing getting out of bed immediately during the middle of the day and it will eventually become natural. [1] That never worked for me, but it might work for some. I've had success waking up to music and then slowly but surely rousing myself while the music plays. Basically, I don't hit the alarm. First, I turn on the light next to my bed. Then I start moving my arms and legs. Then I sit up and just sit there with my back against the bed rest. Shortly thereafter, I'm awake enough to take a shower.

Cold showers will wake you in a hurry, but they are also quite painful. What I do is just turn the water to cold right before I get out. Those 10 seconds do more than any amount of caffeine could.

But why wake up early?

There's a popular book out called *The Miracle Morning* that goes through all of the benefits of an early morning routine.

1. Steve Pavlina, "How to Get Up Right Away When Your Alarm Goes Off", StevePavlina.com, http://www.stevepavlina.com/blog/2006/04/how-to-get-up-right-away-when-your-alarm-goes-off/, April 25, 2006

Its fans are quite avid and with good reason. Most of us live very busy lives and it's hard to fit in that Quadrant 2 stuff (important but not urgent). As the book's author Hal Enrond puts it, "In order to stop settling for less than you deserve… you must first dedicate time each day to becoming the person you need to be." [2]

But once our days get started, there's usually a barrage of things to do as well as distractions and the like. Plus we get tired and begin to lose our focus. Procrastination sets in. "I will do those important things tomorrow, after all, they aren't urgent."

Important things like exercise, planning, prayer, meditation or practicing at some craft or hobby. These things often hit the backburner. The morning, before work and the tasks of the day is the perfect time to take them on. So becoming an early riser is key to making these Quadrant 2 activities a priority in your life.

2. Hal Enrond, *The Miracle Morning*, Hal Elrod International Inc., Copyright 2014, Pg. 3

12

Meditation

Most of us live stressful and busy lives, which is why waking up so early to take care of the important but not urgent this is so, well, important. One of the things I would recommend to put in that morning is a time to meditate. Meditation allows us to unwind from the stress, anxiety and frustration of the past day. Indeed, meditation actually changes how your brain functions. One study had subjects receive brain scans while meditating and it showed "meditation increased activity in the brain regions used for paying attention and making decisions." [1]

Furthermore, it noted that practice makes perfect,

> *While the subjects meditated inside the MRI, the researchers periodically blasted them with disturbing noises. Among the experienced meditators, the noise had less effect on the brain areas involved in emotion and decision-making than among novice meditators. Among meditators with more than 40,000 hours of lifetime practice, these areas were hardly affected at all.*

40,000 hours may be a bit ridiculous, but the psychological

---

1. Brain scans show meditation changes minds, increases attention", University of Wisconsin Madison, http://www.news.wisc.edu/13890, June 25, 2007

benefits of meditating are well understood. As the clinical psychiatrist Rebecca Gladding explains at *Psychology Today,*

> *[Meditation] makes a huge difference in how you approach life, how personally you take things and how you interact with others. It enhances compassion, allows you to see things more clearly (including yourself) and creates a sense of calm and centeredness that is indescribable. There really is no substitute.* [2]

This one has been a struggle for me. I've often found excuses to put it aside in favor of other things, especially when I fall into the trap of not waking up early. But when I have made it a priority, I've certainly noticed a reduction in stress. I would definitely recommend adding it to your morning routine, or, if failing that, sometime else throughout the day.

2. Rebecca Gladding, "This Is Your Brain on Meditation", *Psychology Today,* https://www.psychologytoday.com/blog/use-your-mind-change-your-brain/201305/is-your-brain-meditation, May 22, 2013

13

Quit Smoking the Easy Way

If you're a smoker, you're probably like me; you never wanted to be one and never thought I would get hooked on the damn things. I think I had my first cigarette when I was 17 and became an official smoker sometime around the age of 22. During the next six years, I tried to quit dozens of times. Occasionally, I would quit for a month or two — and then I'd have a stressful day, and fall right back into the trap.

Then I read a book and quit instantly.

The book is *The Easy Way to Stop Smoking* by the Allen Carr. What Allen Carr does is explains why the normal methods of quitting almost always fail. They fail because they are based on willpower. Paul Popov, someone who successfully quit with Allen Carr's approach, describes the problem with the normal willpower method,

> *Willpower is, contrary to the popular belief, a finite resource, which means that there is a fair possibility that a series of negative events will crush it and your no-smoking story will end in something they call "extinction burst."* [1]

1. Paul Popov, "Why You Need More Than Willpower To Quit Smoking", *Thought Cata-*

Willpower is finite. So what Allen Carr did was turn the whole thing around. Instead of asking "why shouldn't we smoke?" he asks "why do we smoke?" Everyone already knows smoking is terrible for your health, [2] costs a fortune and makes you stink and feel lethargic. I think it's quite obvious that people don't smoke for these reasons.

Allen Carr notes that there are only two reasons people smoke:

1. Nicotine Addiction
2. The Brainwashing

Let's start with the addiction. While nicotine is extremely addictive, it's an extremely weak addiction. The withdrawal pangs are almost entirely illusory. As Carr notes,

> There is no physical pain in the withdrawal from nicotine. It is merely a slightly empty, restless feeling, the feeling that something isn't quite right, or that something is missing... [3]

And furthermore,

> Most smokers go all night without a cigarette. The withdrawal "pangs" do not even wake them up. Many smokers will leave the bedroom before they

log, http://thoughtcatalog.com/paul-popov/2014/05/why-you-need-more-than-willpower-to-quit-smoking/, May 8, 2014

2. In case you need reminding, see "Health Effects of Cigarette Smoking", Centers for Disease Control and Prevention, http://www.cdc.gov/tobacco/data_statistics/fact_sheets/health_effects/effects_cig_smoking/index.htm, Accessed May 2, 2015

3. Allen Carr, The Easy Way to Stop Smoking, Sterling Publishing Co., Inc., Copyright 2004, Pg. 24

light that first cigarette; many will have breakfast first. Increasingly people don't smoke in their homes and won't have that first cigarette until they are in the car on the way to work... These smokers have eight or maybe ten hours without a cigarette—going through withdrawal all the while, but it doesn't seem to bother them. [4]

So why do we smoke? It's certainly not because of the petty withdrawal pangs. The reason is because we think we're giving up something precious and that feeling of deprivations causes almost all of the terrible withdrawal pangs quitters experience. This is where the brainwashing comes in. The brainwashing makes us think that the cigarette is actually something quite good. We think the cigarette relieves stress and boredom and helps us concentrate and relax. And while these are illusions, they can have a powerful effect on us if we believe them. After all, the mind can actually make the body physically sick. [5]

For example, a smoker we'll say "I smoke to alleviate boredom." But honestly, what could be more boring than a cigarette? Indeed, many of these claims are actually contradictory. Carr again,

The smoker himself will decide when [he smokes] and it tends to be on four types of occasions...

4. Ibid., Pg. 34
5. See for example, Eric Yosomono, "The 5 Strangest Ways Your Mind Can Get Your Body Sick", *Cracked*, http://www.cracked.com/article_19209_the-5-strangest-ways-your-mind-can-get-your-body-sick.html, May 27, 2011

Boredom/Concentration-Two complete opposites!

Stress/Relaxation-Two Complete opposites!

What magic drug can suddenly reverse the very effect it had twenty minutes earlier? [6]

The very first instruction in the book is to smoke until you finish. This allows Carr to obliterate every possible excuse you have for smoking and let you come to the realization that smoking adds nothing to your life, but instead takes away a massive amount.

So once I realized that the withdrawal pangs were a joke and that nicotine added nothing, quitting was almost embarrassingly easy for me.

And this has certainly been the experience of many others. I bought the book about two years ago the book had over 1000 ratings on *Amazon.com* and still had a five star rating! That is something I have never seen for a book with that many ratings. And the few negative reviews seem to have missed the mark entirely. For example,

> *I wish this book were true. Unfortunately, it is wishful thinking. It does not take into account the actual physical symptoms of quitting smoking. It assumes that all physical ills are psychological, which they aren't. I am so disappointed with both the book and the reviews.* [7]

6. Allen Carr, *The Easy Way to Stop Smoking*, Sterling Publishing Co., Inc., Copyright 2004, Pg. 53
7. Jla, "false advertising", customer review on Amazon.com, http://www.amazon.com/

This, of course, ignores the fact that Carr demonstrated that the physical side effects of nicotine withdrawal are extremely mild. How exactly, if the "symptoms of quitting smoking" are so bad, do we sleep through the night without them bothering us in the slightest?

Furthermore, other forms of quitting don't work anywhere close to as well (I can certainly attest to that). For example, it's correctly claimed that nicotine replacement therapy doubles the chance of success. But then again, it doubles your chances only to about 10 percent. [8] On the other hand, a study in the *Internal Archives of Occupational Environmental Health* showed Allen Carr's seminars to have a 12 month success rate of 51.4 percent! [9]

He also offers a money back guarantee at his live seminars, and claims that less than 10 percent end up requesting such a refund. Given how it seems that Carr's message flew over the heads of those who failed, how many of those that failed just didn't take the book (or seminar) to heart?

So if you are trying to quit smoking, do yourself a favor and give *The Easy Way to Stop Smoking* a try. To see more, view his website at www.allencarr.com. [10]

gp/customer-reviews/R2BCAY08MHBH9S/
ref=cm_cr_pr_rvw_ttl?ie=UTF8&ASIN=0973468408, June 20, 2012
8. See John R. Polito, "Is Nicotine Replacement Therapy The Smoker's Last Best Hope?", *Why Quit*, http://whyquit.com/whyquit/A_NRT.html, November 14, 2000
9. H. Moshammer and M. Neuberger, "Long term success of short smoking cessation seminars by occupational health care", *Journal of Addictive Behaviors*, http://www.ncbi.nlm.nih.gov/pubmed/17097816, November 13, 2006
10. Author's Note: Neither I nor Thought Catalog are affiliated with Allen Carr or his organization in any way. I'm just a very happy customer.

14

Shortcut Your Willpower

For those of you who aren't smokers, there's still something to learn from Allen Carr's method; namely that willpower is finite and cannot be relied up on for goals that requires avoiding temptations in the long term.

Willpower is like gasoline and we can only go so long before we run out. Psychologist Roy Baumeister demonstrated this quite clearly with what he calls the Radish Experiment,

> *When the college students walked into Baumeister's laboratory, they were already hungry because they'd been fasting… The experimental subjects sat down at a table with several culinary choices: warm cookies, some pieces of chocolate, and a bowl of radishes. Some students were invited to eat the cookies and candy. The unlucky ones were assigned to "the radish condition": no treats, just raw radishes.*

> *…the researchers left the students alone with the radishes and the cookies, and observed them through a small, hidden window. The ones in the radish condition clearly struggled with the temptation. Many gazed longingly at the cookies before steeling down to bite reluctantly into a radish.*

Some of them picked up a cookie and smelled it,
savoring the pleasure of freshly baked chocolate...

[Afterward] the students were taken to another room
and given geometry puzzles to work on... in fact, the
puzzles were insoluble. The test was to see how long
they'd work before giving up. The students who'd been
allowed to eat chocolate chip cookies and candy typi-
cally worked on the puzzles for about twenty min-
utes... The sorely tempted radish eaters, though, gave
up in just eight minutes. [1]

In other words, the radish eaters had had their willpower drained whereas the cookie eaters had a full tank. If we constantly desire something, eventually we'll cave.

You see, our brains aren't the logical, clear-thinking computers we often would like them to be. We are creatures of habit and our brains are organs of habit. The way to shortcut our willpower is to reduce the amount of time we need to use it. Then, during the few occasions we need it, we'll have a full tank of it to use.

This obviously doesn't mean we shouldn't work to improve the amount of willpower we have. Baumeister noted one experiment where participants were required to work on their posture for two weeks. This simple task caused a spillover and "...their scores on the self-control tests went up." [2]

But I would recommend going at willpower from both sides. Yes, try to increase the size of your tank, but also align

1. Roy Baumeister and John Tierney, Willpower, Penguin Books Ltd., Copyright 2011, Pg. 22-23
2. Ibid., Pg. 131

your life so that there is less need to avoid temptation. This involves being cognizant of our habits.

Habits are by no means unbreakable. Indeed, sometimes it takes little more than a change of scenery. A very interesting case of this is heroin addiction in the Vietnam War. From the book *Change Anything*,

> *...In the 1970's [the] U.S. government waited for sixty-nine thousand heroin-addicted soldiers to return form the very site that got them addicted in the first place—Vietnam. Leaders worried that hospitals and jails would be overwhelmed by the problems associated with these addicted troops. But the problems never came. In fact, 88 percent of those who were diagnosed as 'seriously addicted' kicked the habit shortly after leaving Vietnam.* [3]

A change of scenery might be the answer, but it's often too drastic or not practical. When it comes to the habits we have in a more normal setting, Charles Duhigg in his book *The Power of Habit*, outlines the four major steps to identifying a habit and thereby changing it.

– *Identify the routine*

– *Experiment with rewards*

3. Kerry Patterson, Joseph Grenny, David Maxfield, Ron McMillian, and David Switzler, *Change Anything*, VitalSmarts, LLC., Copyright 2011, Pg. 193

– Isolate the cue

– Have a plan [4]

He then gives an example,

> *...Let's say you have a bad habit, like I did when I started researching this book, of going to the cafeteria and buying a chocolate chip cookie every afternoon... the first step is figuring out the routine... [Then] what's the cue for the routine? Is it hunger? Boredom?... To figure this out, you'll need to do a little experimentation.*

> *To figure out which cravings are driving particular habits, it's useful to experiment with different rewards. On the first day of your experiment, when you feel the urge to go to the cafeteria and buy a cookie, adjust your routine so it delivers a different reward. For instance, instead of walking to the cafeteria, go outside, walk around the block and then go back to your desk without eating anything. The next day, go to the cafeteria and buy a donuts or a candy bar, and eat it at your desk. The next day... buy an apple, and eat it while chatting with your friends.* [5]

4. Charles Duhigg, *The Power of Habit*, Random House Publishing Group, Copyright 2012, Pg. 276
5. Charles Duhigg, *The Power of Habit*, Random House Publishing Group, Copyright 2012, Pg. 277-278

He then notes that,

Experiments have shown that almost all habitual cues fit into one of five categories: Location, Time, Emotional State, Other People, [and the] Immediately Preceding Action. [6]

So take note of each of these whenever you're following through with a habit you would like to change. Then make a plan. He found out in this case that he was actually craving a distraction, so at that time he would instead spend 10 minutes talking to a friend. Habits do take some time to make or break, however. As the psychologist Jeremy Dean observed, "On average, habit formation [takes] 66 days," [7] although it varies from thing to thing. So habits will take at least some willpower to change, but then you will have reached a level of "automaticity" that should keep it going.

Now, taking on your bad habits is great, but it's also important to put yourself on autopilot as much as possible. For example, in one study, participants were asked to eat from a bowl of soup. But the bowls had a tube placed into the bottom that continuously filled the bowl as the person ate. The people with these self-filling bowls ate over 70 percent more soup than the control group. [8] What's the lesson? Something as simple as having smaller plates and bowls in your home can help with portion control. Here are some other ideas,

6. Ibid, pg. 283
7. Jeremy Dean, Making Habits, *Breaking Habits*, Da Capo Press, Copyright 2013, Pg. 6
8. Brian Wansink, James E. Painter and Jill North, "Bottomless Bowls: Visual Cues of Portion Size May Influence Intake", Obesity Research, Volume 13 No 1, January 2005

- Don't buy junk food at the store to keep in your home, make yourself go out to get it if you want it so much.
- Don't keep a television in your bedroom, or better yet, get rid of it entirely.
- Eat more foods that are low on the glycemic index to better regulate your blood sugar and feel hungry less (i.e. less sugars and carbohydrates). [9]
- And of course, if you are a smoker, buy Allen Carr's book or attend his seminar.

But I would say it goes even deeper than merely aligning your life with good habits to avoid depleting your willpower. You should also align your thoughts. This requires metacognition, or thinking about your thinking. Why do you want certain things? Why do you naturally behave the way you do?

I would pose this question to you. Why does a pack of Starburst taste better than a Honeycrisp apple?

Perhaps it's just a subjective matter of opinion, but it would seem to me that many people try very hard to avoid eating candy, but very few try or have any difficulty avoiding fruit. Think hard, why do you like candy more?

I would argue that you probably don't. The reason you want candy is probably the same reason I wanted cigarettes when I was addicted to nicotine. The fact you shouldn't eat candy makes it look like it's on the other side of the fence. You know, the side with the greener grass. That sense of depriva-

9. Stephanie Watson, "The Glycemic Index Diet", *Web MD*, http://www.webmd.com/diet/glycemic-index-diet, December 16, 2013

tion makes you want it. Whereas there is no such restriction on fruit, so who cares?

But once we realize that this is the reason, it becomes absurd. And all of a sudden it becomes easy to substitute candy with fruit in order to satisfy our sweet tooth.

Go through all sorts of junk food and do this same test. Does soda really taste good? Again, it's all subjective, of course, but try holding a gulp of Coke or Pepsi in your mouth for more than a few seconds. It fizzles and then starts to burn. In fact, it actually doesn't taste that good once you actually analyze it.

So don't drink it.

Once we don't want the things that tempt us, willpower becomes kind of irrelevant.

This same sort of metacognition can be done with all sorts of things. If you don't like working out, but enjoy say, playing basketball, play basketball to work out. If you don't like cleaning your house (who does?), then listen to music while you do it. Life should be enjoyable, so make it that way!

You can even look at your relationships this way. We'll go with the stereotypes here, but let's say a man and woman are dating. Today, she would like to go shopping and he hates shopping. Tomorrow night, he wants to watch the football game, but she hates football.

Should these two lovers agonize through all of this just to spend time with each other? Sometime perhaps, but how about today, she goes shopping with her friends and then in the night they can hang out together doing something they both like. Then tomorrow, they can hang out together again and then he can go watch the game with his friends while she departs to do something she would rather do.

Relationships shouldn't be about suffering each other's company. Sometimes it's necessary, but overall, time spent with each other should be well spent. The more we feel deprived because of someone, the more likely we are to resent that person. In other words, you should align your relationships as best as possible to serve both of you instead of just spending time together because that's what you're supposed to do when you're in a relationship.

Shortcut your willpower and everything becomes easier, especially the hard things that require a full tank.

Part 4

Relationships

15

Give and You Shall Receive

It's said that you can catch more flies with honey than with vinegar. Indeed, the best way to get what you want in life, particularly from your relationships, is to give it first. People, generally speaking, will act as a mirror. The way you treat other people will be reflected right back in the way they treat you.

Zig Ziglar may have put it best, "If you go out looking for friends, you're going to find they are very scarce. If you go out to be a friend, you'll find them everywhere." [1]

Indeed, the mere act of smiling (genuinely) when you meet someone gets things off on the right path. Make people feel appreciated. As Leil Lowland advises, "…look at the other person's face for a second. Pause. Soak in their persona. Then let a big, warm, responsive smile flood over your face and overflow into your eyes. It will engulf the recipient like a warm wave." [2] And then she will, in all likelihood, smile back at you.

Robert Cialdini calls this the "rule of reciprocation." He describes an experiment that illustrates this,

---

1. "Zig Ziglar>Quotes", *Good Reads*, http://www.goodreads.com/author/quotes/50316.Zig_Ziglar, Accessed May 2, 2015
2. Leil Lowland, *How to Talk to Anyone*, Harper Collins Publishers, Copyright 2008, Pg. 8

A subject who participated in the study found himself rating, along with another subject, the quality of some paintings as part of an experiment on "art appreciation. The other subject—we can call him Joe—was only posing as a fellow subject… In some cases, Joe did a small, unsolicited favor for the true subject. During a short rest period, he left the room for a couple of minutes and returned with two bottles of Coca-Cola, one for the subject and one for himself… In other cases, Joe did not provide the subject with a favor; he simply returned from the two-minute break empty-handed.

Later on, after the paintings had all been rated and the experimenter had momentarily left the room, Joe asked the subject to do him a favor. He indicated that he was selling raffle tickets for a new car and that if he sold the most tickets, he would win a fifty-dollar prize. Joe's request was for the subject to buy some raffle tickets at twenty-five cents apiece: 'Any would help, the more the better.' The major finding of the study concerns the number of tickets subjects purchased from Joe under the two conditions… Apparently feeling that they owed him something, these subjects bought twice as many tickets as the subjects who had not been given the prior favor. [3]

3. Robert Cialdini, *Influence*, William Morrow and Company Inc., Copyright 1993, Pg. 21

Sales expert Bob Burg relates this same concept to business,

> *Continually look for opportunities to refer busi-*
> *ness whenever you can... There is simply no better*
> *way to get someone to want to do something for*
> *you, than first doing something for them... First*
> *they will most likely appreciate what you did for*
> *them. Human nature being what it is, most people*
> *are genuinely nice and appreciative and will want*
> *to give you something back in return.* [4]

While this is certainly applicable to business and negotiations, it is not about doing something in order to get something in return per se. It's more about being someone and doing what such a person would do and being treated likewise in kind. This is not about false flattery or gifts with strings attached. Such deception will only work in the short run, particularly regarding relationships.

We are all selfish to one degree or another. Even when we give to charity, is it not that good feeling of knowing that we've done something nice for someone else that makes us want to give? When we think in terms of a rational self-inter-est—versus mindless selfishness—we begin to approach our relationships proactively.

Stephen Covey gives an excellent example of this in his famous book *The Seven Habits of Highly Effective People,*

> *At one seminar where I was speaking on the con-*
> *cept of proactivity, a man came up and*

4. Bob Burg, *Endless Referrals*, McGraw-Hill Professional, Copyright 2006, Pg. 55

said "Stephen, I like what you're saying. But every situation is so different. Look at my marriage. I'm really worried. My wife and I just don't have the same feelings for each other we used to have. I guess I just don't lover her anymore and she doesn't love me. What can I do?"

"The feeling isn't there anymore?" I asked.

"That's right," he reaffirmed. "And we have three children we're really concerned about. What do you suggest?"

"Love her," I replied.

"You don't understand. The feeling of love just isn't there."

"Then love her. If the feeling isn't there, that's a good reason to love her."

"But how do you love when you don't love?"

"My friend, love is a verb. Love—the feeling—is a fruit of love, the verb. So love her. Serve her. Sacrifice. Listen to her. Empathize. Appreciate. Affirm her. Are you willing to do that?" [5]

Feelings are a fleeting thing. For any sort of long term friendship or relationship, it requires much more than just the nat-

5. Stephen Covey, *The Seven Habits of Highly Effective People*, Simon and Schuster, Copyright 1989, Pg. 79-80

ural actions our whims lead us toward. Long term success in relationships requires a proactive approach—an approach that doesn't come naturally to us. Indeed, it's often like George Costanza in *Seinfeld*, where we must do the opposite of what we feel we want to. We may be angry, but speaking in anger will only make the other person defensive and angry as well.

This, of course, doesn't mean we should be a pushover. Going against the grain certainly isn't weak. It takes strength to bite one's tongue or give without any assurance that one will receive anything in return. But that is the foundation of good friendships and relationships.

16

Avoid Arguing

"...I have come to the conclusion that there is only one way under high heaven to get the best of an argument—and that is to avoid it." [1] That is the advice of the great Dale Carnegie and who am I to argue with it.

This is, again, not to say that one should be a pushover. There is a difference between having a disagreement and having an argument. If you believe something and someone else disagrees, you shouldn't change your mind unless that person persuades you. But that doesn't mean you need to argue with him.

To the contrary, if someone disagrees with you, the only way to possibly convince him is *not* to argue. People often associate their own opinions with themselves as people. The two become intertwined. And virtually everyone thinks they are a decent person with good intentions. Dale Carnegie illustrates the point early on by describing "Two Gun" Crowley, a notorious murderer who wrote a letter shortly before he was finally shot by police that read, "Under my coat is a weary heart, but a kind one – one that would do nobody any harm." [2] Indeed, a serial killer seriously believed he "would do nobody any harm." What do you think the average person

1. Dale Carnegie, *How to Win Friends and Influence People*, Simon and Schuster Inc., Copyright 1964 Pg. 116
2. Ibid., Pg. 22

thinks about themselves then? Everyone is the hero of their own story; it would be wise to remember that.

Let me illustrate this with a personal example. My brother is a property manager and has become an expert in tenant relations. Immediately after he took over as property manager, a lawsuit for $3500 was dropped on his desk. It came from a tenant who had been evicted. She claimed that several maintenance items had been left unfixed and as a result, some of her property was damaged. We had tried to repair them, but she had changed out the lock (which is not allowed in the lease) and we had had trouble getting ahold of her. Then our previous manager let it fall to the back burner. The tenant refused to pay (at least so she said) and then an eviction was filed.

This cluster of mistakes was in the past though. So my brother had to deal with things as they stood. He finally got ahold of her and my brother did that the great negotiating book *Getting to Yes* suggested, "Separate the people from the problem." [3]

He started off as follows,

> *I know you're mad about what happened. I haven't dealt with this situation so I'm a little in the dark. Please tell me what happened from your point of view.*

Friendly and validating without conceding anything. She explained all of her grievances. In fact, this was the first

---

3. Roger Fisher and William Ury, *Getting to Yes*, Penguin Books, Copyright 1991, Pg. 10

time my brother had even heard that she claimed to withhold rent because of the maintenance issues.

Now at this point, my brother could have attacked her reasoning: "We sent out our maintenance guy twice. You wouldn't answer our calls. You put a lock on our door in violation of the lease," etc. Or he could have made it easy for himself and simply said, "Please sue us and make my life a living hell." They're all the same.

Remember, arguing is useless.

Instead, my brother got on her team. He was the good guy. There was a bad guy in this case, which was some combination of the past and the previous manager. Other times it might be the lease or the law.

"I can't change the past, so we should find the best way to move forward," my brother said. Then her concerns and fears started coming out: she didn't have much money, she didn't have a new place to live and it was hard to find one with an eviction on her record.

Always listen. We spend so much time talking we forget to listen. And no one listens in an argument. In this case, her supposedly damaged property was not among her concerns.

After learning what was bothering her, my brother responded,

> *OK, well it looks like what you really want to do is move on and find a new quality place to live, and I think I can help you come up with the best solution for your situation. You can continue to sue us. That's an option. I think it would be better to try and work something out, though.*

She held plenty of responsibility for what happened, but she also had the right to be upset. To say that suing us was a stupid idea is to call her stupid, no matter what euphemism you use. What this did was put him on her side and validate her opinion even if there was a disagreement. Indeed, in some ways they were on the same side; she would have probably lost the lawsuit and got nothing. And no one ever wins by being sued. The time and money to defend yourself are simply not worth it.

He offered to pay her back her deposit, write a letter for future landlords explaining the situation and open up the court case to satisfy the judgment and get the eviction off her record. In this case, the deposit was a mere $350.

While this story is about business, you can easily see how this could relate to relationships with your spouse, children, parents, siblings, friends and coworkers. Have you ever worked something out while arguing with your wife or husband? What about your father or mother? Close friend perhaps?

The only way to get someone to do something, other than force, is to get them to want to do it. If you attack their position, it gets misinterpreted (or correctly interpreted) as attacking that person directly. Thus, your target must dig their heels in to defend their own self esteem (the actual subject of the argument actually doesn't matter much).

It's hard to change someone's mind, but it's impossible to do it with arguing. But you will damage the relationship substantially by trying. So make it easy on yourself and just avoid arguing.

17

Honesty (Again)

Just like fear is alleviated through honesty, relationships are strengthened from it, within reason of course. This does not mean, say, that it is unwise to say something like, "They both look great, but I think I like the other one a little bit more" instead of "Yeah honey, you know, it's funny you should ask because you kind of do look fat in that." What it does mean is that you shouldn't let grievances fester into a rot.

Sometime back, I had had a large disagreement with my brother and father over the way we were handling our business. We finally sat down and hashed it all out (without arguing, at least as best we could). I remember being rather fired up afterward. But then, it faded. Shortly thereafter, the actual subject matter of a fairly long-standing disagreement was hard to remember. In fact, it was only by recalling the actual steps to alleviate the problem that I could remember exactly what the dispute was over.

Not every disagreement can be fixed so easily, but these issues don't generally get better by hiding in the shadows. Instead they begin to saw at us and consume more and more mental energy. We begin to perceive the person who is doing whatever displeases us as more and more sinister. Their motives become something close to evil until we actually hear what they are. Then, all of a sudden, they become quite understandable, if not completely justifiable.

We only get our side of the story when these things are left in our own mind.

Brad Blanton recommends what he calls "radical honesty." He believes we all hide our true selves in "roles" that we pretend to play,

> *Coming out from behind our roles permits us to look behind the roles of others. Because we can see more clearly, the threat of other people, posing in their roles, fades. Once we come out from behind our pose, what used to scare us about other people doesn't scare us anymore... The person capable of intimacy—that is, the person capable of telling the truth—still has roles to play, but is no longer trapped by them. The integrated person behind the role no longer has anything to hide, and can relate freely to the being he knows is hidden behind the roles others are playing.* [1]

Blanton is certainly more extreme than I would be. Indeed, I have work to do to even get to where I believe I should be in this regard. And I would caution more discretion that I'm sure Blanton would. But it's certainly true that if we aren't open with others about ourselves, they can never befriend or love or even tolerate us for anything other than what we are trying to project.

1. Brad Blanton, *Radical Honesty*, Dell Publishing, Copyright 1975, Pg. 48

Thereby, every relationship we have is, to one degree or another, false. This will lead to nothing more than a bunch of shallow and unsatisfying relationships. Being honest is a pre-requisite for any relationship.

18

Addition by Subtraction

An article in *Business By Day* makes the claim that the time an employer should fire someone is the first time you think about it. [1] OK, even that article admits that may be a bit too quick, but there's certainly a point there.

My father told me that in the 31 years of being in business, he has never regretted letting someone go. Well, that's not completely accurate; he's usually had regrets after letting someone go — he almost always regrets not having let them go earlier.

My experience in business has, unfortunately, been the same. So has that of every other owner I have talked to.

Sometimes the person was terrible at their job, sometimes he or she just wasn't a good fit. I've seen people we've let go make it somewhere else, even when their performance for us was miserable. But the mistake employers make is almost always the same; holding on too long.

Now, friendships and relationships are not like that of business colleagues, bosses and subordinates. Employees may be trying to perform well, but your friends and family are not performing for you.

That being said, those around us have a major influence on

1. Rick Day, "THE BEST TIME TO FIRE SOMEONE IS THE FIRST TIME YOU THINK ABOUT IT", *Business by Day*, http://www.businessbyday.com/the-best-time-to-fire-someone-is-the-first-time-you-think-about-it/, March 31, 2014

our own behavior and attitudes. Indeed, psychologists have coined the term "social proof" to describe, as *Wikipedia* does, the "...psychological phenomenon where people assume the actions of others in an attempt to reflect correct behavior for a given situation." [2] In other words, you begin to become the company you keep.

I don't mean to imply that you should discard friends and family left and right if these people have some undesirable flaw. Everyone has some undesirable flaws.

But what I do mean to say is that one should be very mindful of the company they keep. Don't hold onto a friendship or relationship just because you are afraid to lose it or afraid you can't find another. You can. The grass is not necessarily greener on the other side of the fence, but if the grass is dead where you are, it's probably time to go looking elsewhere.

When to let go is hard to know and writing here from afar, I can give you no advice. I do know that many marriages are left to rot because couples don't love each other (the verb form) and instead argue with each other endlessly. You should always look in the mirror first before making a decision to end a relationship or even a friendship.

But negative people and influences can pull you down and so these influences need to be managed appropriately. Sometimes that simply means letting go.

2. "Social Proof", Wikipedia, http://en.wikipedia.org/wiki/Social_proof, Accessed May 2, 2015

Part 5

Money and Business

19

Avoid Consumer Debt

Albert Einstein once opined that "Compound interest is the eighth wonder of the world. He who understands it, earns it… he who doesn't… pays it." [1]

Why would you want to be the one who pays it? In 2014, American consumers had a gargantuan total of $11.9 trillion dollars in outstanding debt. [2] Fortunately, most of this debt was on things like mortgages and student loans.

Still, Americans had $884.8 billion in credit card debt, which amounts to $15,609 per household. Which is a lot; especially given interest rates on credit cards usually start around 15 percent and then go up.

The principle of debt is rather simple: borrow money now and pay it back in the future, with interest. Thereby, anything bought with debt will cost more than it would have otherwise.

And, with credit card debt, it's a lot more. Something you bought for $100 today will cost something like $115 next year. So incurring this debt better be worth it.

Now, not all debt is bad. The good kind allows one to make a return (financial or otherwise). So, mortgage debt used to

1. Albert Einstein, "Albert Einstein>Quotes>Quotable Quotes", *Good Reads*, http://www.goodreads.com/quotes/76863-compound-interest-is-the-eighth-wonder-of-the-world-he, Accessed May 3, 2015
2. Tim Chen, "American Household Credit Card Debt Statistics: 2015", *Nerd Wallet*, http://www.nerdwallet.com/blog/credit-card-data/average-credit-card-debt-household/, Accessed May 3, 2015

purchase a house would often qualify as good debt because houses will, in the long run, appreciate. And you would still have to rent if you didn't buy a house.

Debt for starting a business or purchasing an investment vehicle can also be good, since the goal is to make more than the cost of repayment. Student loans can be good debt, because we invest in our earning potential and or personal improvement and fulfillment (although the rapidly increasing costs of college seem to be making it less so). Other debts, such as those to pay for medical expenses, may not be good debt, but they are necessary debt.

But then there's the bad kind, which is pretty much everything else. Virtually any debt on a depreciating asset or on something that doesn't allow us to grow as individuals should be qualified as bad debt.

Patience is a virtue, and a lack of patience is quite expensive. It's what economists call "time preference." Effectively, an individual's time preference is the relative value placed on a good now versus at some point in the future. The less time you're willing to wait, the more you'll end up paying because of the interest that will accumulate during that time.

Rent-to-own televisions, computers and even cars are simply transfers of wealth from the impatient to the patient. Bad debt means you are obligating yourself to work in the future to pay off whatever you're buying today.

Why would you make such obligations? The work you do should pay for the present and to build a nest egg for the future, not just allow you to pay off something you've already used up.

What this all boils down to is perhaps the greatest key to success in life: the deferral of gratification.

In the famous Stanford Marshmallow Experiment, [3] young children were given the option of eating one marshmallow immediately or waiting 15 minutes to get two. Most children quickly succumbed to the temptation of the marshmallow and deprived themselves of the second. Only about one-third of them were able to hold out for the second marshmallow.

Many years later, the researchers evaluated how well the students did in life, and those who waited for the second marshmallow did substantially better than those who had not, on a wide range of factors. James Clear describes the results as follows,

> *The children who were willing to delay gratification and waited to receive the second marshmallow ended up having higher SAT scores, lower levels of substance abuse, lower likelihood of obesity, better responses to stress, better social skills as reported by their parents, and generally better scores in a range of other life measures.* [4]

And similar results of this study have been repeatedly replicated. There is no question, the ability to delay gratification is universally regarded as one of the most fundamental skills a

---

3. "Stanford Marshmallow Experiment", Wikipedia, http://en.wikipedia.org/wiki/Stanford_marshmallow_experiment, Accessed May 3, 2015
4. James Clear, "40 Years of Stanford Research Found That People With This One Quality Are More Likely to Succeed", *JamesClear.com*, http://jamesclear.com/delayed-gratification

successful person can have. And, thereby, it's one of the most important skills to nurture in yourself.

So the moral of the story is simple: Consumer debt represents the first marshmallow.

And yes, this isn't the easiest thing to do given the smorgasbord of cool, new consumer products deftly marketed everywhere along with the massive amounts of money various companies spend in advertising. But it's a temptation you must fight to avoid.

In the end, building a nest egg and having enough disposable income to do what you want in life involves saving money, not paying through the nose for things that will become all but worthless by the time they are paid off.

Even a new car loses more than 10 percent of its value the moment you drive it off the lot! [5]

The more bad debt a person has, the worse his or her credit score will be (and, the more likely he or she is to default), making it that much harder to acquire good debt and get it at a good interest rate.

Going into debt because there's no other choice is one thing; otherwise, debt should only be used as an investment. I strongly recommend splitting debt into the good and bad categories and leaving the bad type for good. Make it a rule instead of a recommendation. Even auto loans should be avoided, if possible.

Bad debt, which includes virtually all consumer debt, leaves you running just to stay in the same place. Avoid it like the plague.

5. "Depreciation Infographic: How fast Does My New Car Lose Value?", *Edmunds*, http://www.edmunds.com/car-buying/how-fast-does-my-new-car-lose-value-infographic.html, September 24, 2010

20

Negotiating 101

Back when I was in college, I had a class on negotiations, and one of the main projects was called "collecting no's." Basically, we had to get rejected 10 times. Each request had to be realistic, legal and to someone who didn't know you were asking it as part of an assignment. The goal was to collect at least 10 "no's" and write them each down and turn in that notebook. The point was that by collecting "no's" you could break down the fear of rejection.

Salespeople will sometimes talk as if they have to go through X number of "no's" to get a "yes" based on what percentage of their leads they actually convert. So every "no" — while technically accomplishing nothing — psychologically feels like moving forward.

Such assignments are helpful, but they don't finish the job by any means. Getting rejected still sucks. But generally speaking, it's the fear of that rejection that's the worst thing. I'm not talking about being rejected by a spouse or parent or someone really close to you, but in the smaller things. And with those things, it really shouldn't matter if you're rejected. After all, what harm is it really for someone to say no to you?

While it may be easy to tell yourself that, it's a lot harder to actually feel that way. I certainly have by no means mastered this, but I can say it helps to consciously remind yourself beforehand of how little it will matter in a month. Imagine detaching yourself from the situation and seeing it as a third party, neutral observer. Take the emotion out of it, as well as the potential for hurt feelings or embarrassment. If they get offended or angry or reject you, who cares?

What would that third party observer think? Well, such a person would probably be bored out of their mind. Watching two people negotiate a deal you have no stake in (and aren't trying to learn from) is about as interesting as watching paint dry.

And, of course, each time it gets easier. So keep at it, and that sense of calm during negotiations will come, at least to a large extent. If you don't have much experience negotiating, however, you will just have to accept the butterflies. It's best not to try to overload yourself with various negotiating techniques and what not to do when approaching negotiating early on.

Instead, focus on the key components until you master them. And they boil down to three things:

- Ask for what you want
- Always be willing to walk away
- First build rapport

Let's start with asking for what you want. I've noticed time and time again that most things are negotiable and just asking, "Do you have any flexibility on price?" is all it takes to get at least some sort of discount.

Some time back, my father was trying to purchase a house and had reached his bottom line. Unfortunately, he and the seller were still $10,000 apart. He was stuck at $170,000, and she was at $180,000.

Earlier in the conversation, however, the seller had mentioned how her son needed a new cell phone. Well, my dad just happened to have an extra one (a phone that he was going to give to me, by the way). All of a sudden, a solution appeared.

"How about this? I happen to have an extra cell phone—what if I throw it in if you can come down to $170,000? Does that work?"

And she said yes.

One cellphone for $10,000.

This story obviously highlights the importance of building rapport, but it also shows how critical it is to simply ask for what you want. I've heard many real estate investors say that if you're not embarrassed about your first offer, you're offering too much. And there's certainly a lot of truth in that much of the time. But a better way to think of it is this: just ask for what you want.

Yes, the offer was kind of ridiculous, but what was the harm in it? After all, my dad had reached his bottom line. So his choices were to either find a creative (or ridiculous) solution or walk away from the deal.

And that leads us to the second key; always be willing to walk away. Sometime back, I was traveling in South America with a good friend of mine who is fluent in Spanish. My Spanish at the time was *no bueno,* so I was fairly reliant on him when it came to communicating with the locals.

Anyways, I had somehow forgotten my sunglasses back in the States, and so we walked to one of the local shops to buy a new pair. I picked up the pair and asked how much. "Treinta mil pesos" (thirty thousand) the shopkeeper told me. ¡Un precio para un gringo! My friend said (in English) to ask how much he would come down. He offered a token discount. Then my friend told me to set the sunglasses down and begin to walk away. So I did. The guy grabbed my arm and cut his price substantially. "Ask for more," said my friend.

At the end of the day, I bought the sunglasses for thirteen thousand pesos, less than half of what he originally asked for.

Such bartering is par for the course in Latin America, but it highlights a major lesson: The power to walk away is crucial. In some ways, by itself this defeats the fear of rejection. If you're willing to walk away, what can a "no" really do to you? Regardless, it is of the utmost importance to never be a motivated buyer (or seller for that matter).

Any participant who is not willing to walk away is at an enormous disadvantage and will get the short end of the stick almost every time.

The third thing is to build rapport. Don't immediately go into the negotiating, but first talk to and genuinely be interested in the other person. Negotiations are not battles, either you can find an agreement that works, or you bid each other good day and move on. "Don't bargain over positions" but rather their interests (not what they're asking for necessarily, but what they actually want to get out of it) as the negotiating book *Getting To Yes* puts it. [1] By coming at the negotiation as partners rather than adversaries, a wide variety of options can be evaluated and, potentially, a win/win solution can be found.

---

1. Roger Fisher and William Ury, *Getting to Yes*, Penguin Books, Copyright 1991, Pg. 3

Negotiating is not an easy thing to master (and I certainly haven't done it). But as far as the foundation goes, asking for what you want, being willing to walk away and a little rapport building can put you in the top 10 percent of negotiators out there.

21

Advanced Negotiating: Frames and Anchors

Suppose you received the following two proposals:

> *Problem 1… Imagine that the U.S. is preparing for the outbreak of an unusual Asian disease, which is expected to kill 600 people. Two alternative programs to combat the disease have been proposed. Assume that the exact scientific estimates of the consequences of the programs are as follows:*
>
> *If Program A is adopted, 200 people will be saved.*
>
> *If Program B is adopted, there is a one-third probability that 600 people will be saved and a two-thirds probability that no people will be saved.*
>
> *Which of the two programs do you favor?* [1]

This question comes from Nobel Prize winner Daniel Kahneman's excellent book *Thinking Fast and Slow,* and the survey results showed that 72 percent of respondents preferred

1. Daniel Kahneman, *Thinking Fast and Slow,* Farrar, Straus and Giroux, Copyright 2011, Pg. 436

the more reliable Program A, as opposed to 28 percent who supported Program B. Apparently, people generally think we should take the sure bet and save 200 people rather than roll the dice.

But another group of people were offered two different programs to select between,

> *If Program C is adopted, 400 people will die.*
>
> *If Program D is adopted, there is a one-third probability that nobody will die and a two-thirds probability that 600 people will die.* [2]

I hope you've noticed that these two programs are completely identical to the first two with the only exception being that they are worded slightly differently. Well, what happened? The results flipped. This time 78% supported the roll of the dice and only 22% supported the reliable option.

The bias this question elucidates is that people will gravitate toward things that are framed as gains and away from things that are framed as losses. "Lives saved" is a gain and "people will die" is a loss. This is a consistent cognitive bias our species is stuck with. And if there is one lesson to be learned from psychology, it is that people have intrinsic biases.

As Kahneman and others have shown, people will generally become irrationally aggressive when there is a small chance of winning and irrationally conservative when there is a small chance of losing. In addition, they almost always underes-

---

2. Daniel Kahneman, *Thinking Fast and Slow*, Farrar, Straus and Giroux, Copyright 2011, Pg. 437

timate the cost and time required, instead of the other way around. For example, the Sydney Opera House was supposed to cost $7 million. It ended up costing over $100 million and was finished over 10 years behind schedule. [3] People are overly loss averse and have an irrational fixation on not losing money on any particular transaction (i.e. "I'm into 123 Main street for X dollars, so I need to get at least that out of it if I am going to sell it"). Indeed, the list goes on.

What's so important about these biases is that they make not only what we say, but also the way we frame any sort of interaction with other individuals so important. Two people can say the same thing, and one can be completely effective and one can be completely ineffective in conveying it. Someone who highlights losses will be less effective than someone who highlights gains. Someone who comes off mean-spirited will be less effective than someone who comes off empathetic and builds rapport with the buyer or seller.

To use an example from our office, our former bookkeeper used to complain about virtually everything, much of it admittedly legitimate. One day, she asked our operations manager why when the manager complained about a problem, people would listen, but when our bookkeeper complained, people seemed to not want to hear it. Our manager's answer was that she tried to provide a potential solution as well. No one just wants to hear about more problems, but if a potential solution is also given, it makes the person more interested in taking that problem on.

So instead of just making your offer out of the blue, provide

---

3. "Sydney Opera House", Wikipedia, http://en.wikipedia.org/wiki/Sydney_Opera_House, Accessed May 3, 2015

a narrative first. Explain why your offer will be low (or why it should be high if you are selling). By making your rationale ahead of time, you have framed the offer. Now it's not some low ball offer, but an offer that makes sense.

In a recent negotiation for an apartment complex, I asked the owner to come to our office to meet with my brother and me. I then framed our offer by explaining the repairs that needed to be done to the property and the assumptions I had to add to his profit and loss statement (for example, he managed himself and so I had to put in a management fee). Then I explained that it needed perform at a certain level (have a certain cap rate for those in real estate) for it to work for us and showed them what offer price that justified.

And we got a discount big enough to justify buying the property.

Another technique that is critical to know is called anchoring. Daniel Kahneman again,

> *...we told participants in the Exploratorium study about environmental damage caused by oil tankers in the Pacific Ocean and asked about their willingness to make an annual contribution 'to save 50,000 offshore Pacific Coast seabirds from small offshore oil spills, until ways are found to prevent spills or require tanker owners to pay for the operation.' This question requires intensity matching: the respondents are asked, in effect, to find the dollar amount of a contribution that matches the intensity of their feelings about the plight of the seabirds. Some of the visitors were*

*first asked an anchoring question, such as "Would
you be willing to pay $5..." before the point-blank
question of how much they would contribute.*

*When no anchor was mentioned, the visitors at
the Exploratorium—generally an environmentally
sensitive crowd—said they were willing to pay
$64, on average. When the anchoring amount was
only $5, contributions averaged $20. When the
anchor was a rather extravagant $400, the will-
ingness to pay rose to an average of $143.* [4]

Think about this example for a moment. The same types of
people, randomly selected, reduced the amount they were
willing to pay by 75 percent when given a low anchor and
more than doubled it when given a high anchor.

Anchoring, as Daniel Kahneman defines it, "occurs when
people consider a particular value for an unknown quantity
before estimating that quantity. What happens is one of the
most reliable and robust results of experimental psychology:
the estimates stay close to the number that people considered—hence the image of an anchor." [5] This can be a very
powerful tool in any negotiation.

Our brains basically have two methods of thinking. In brief,
there's System 1 that could be thought of as our brain's autopilot.
It's for recognizing faces or familiar symbols. Then there's System
2, which is for more deliberate thinking such as math or abstract

4. Daniel Kahneman, *Thinking Fast and Slow*, Farrar, Straus and Giroux, Copyright
2011, Pg. 124-125
5. Ibid., Pg. 119-120

thought. The thing to remember is that System 2 is lazy as all hell. And System 1 is more than willing to oblige System 2 in its never-ending search for new ways to procrastinate.

Anchoring feeds System 1 something to hang onto, which proliferates up to System 2 and influences the rational mind when it comes time to buckle down and do some serious thinking. In fact, what it means is that unlike much of the negotiation advice you may have heard, sometimes it's a good idea to make the first offer.

Many buyers or sellers have a completely unrealistic view of what something is worth (remember, most people are overly optimistic). Anchoring can help remove these delusions of grandeur and increase the odds of actually getting a deal done.

And what if someone uses a ridiculous anchor on you? Kahneman recommends what I would call the Toddler Tantrum method of negotiating,

> *My advice to students when I taught negotiations was that if you think the other side has made an outrageous proposal, you should not come back with an equally outrageous counteroffer, creating a gap that will be difficult to bridge in further negotiations. Instead you should make a scene, storm out or threaten to do so, and make it clear—to yourself as well as the other side—that you will not continue the negotiation with that number on the table.* [6]

6. Daniel Kahneman, *Thinking Fast and Slow*, Farrar, Straus and Giroux, Copyright 2011, Pg. 126

The key here is not disarming the other person, but invalidating the anchor to your own mind.

Much of life is a negotiation and framing and anchoring exist whether you like it or not. There will be frames and anchors floating around every negotiation you are in even if you despise the concept of them. So you better take them into account.

22

The Purposeful Approach

When I first began learning to play the guitar, the whole exercise was little more than a chore. Switching from one chord to the next was a tedious task that took so much time I couldn't play anything that could possibly be confused with an actual song. It took close to a year before the guitar became something that I actually enjoyed to play.

Eventually, though, that all changed. I had finally mastered enough chords that I could play a variety of simple songs. Then I could play those songs easily. Then I could play them slightly more easily. Then, well, nothing. I plateaued into a pleasant mediocrity. All of a sudden, I had accomplished what I wanted and learned to play the guitar—sort of—and enjoyed playing it. But I wasn't getting any better.

I didn't start improving again until I started taking lessons that forced me to actually work at the fundamentals of the guitar in a way that wasn't particularly enjoyable at first, but was ultimately highly rewarding. This is one of dozens of examples of the power of purposeful action over the more natural way we approach things

Gary Keller outlines the difference between what he calls the "entrepreneurial approach" with the "purposeful approach." Here's how he describes the former,

Entrepreneurial is our natural approach. It's seeing something we want to do or that needs to be done and racing off to do it with enthusiasm, energy, and our natural abilities. No matter the task, all natural ability has a ceiling of achievement, a level of productivity and success that eventually tops out. [1]

On the other hand, the purposeful approach may not be as easy or natural, but it leads to spectacularly better results,

Highly productive people don't accept the limitations of their natural approach as the final word on their success. When they hit a ceiling of achievement, they look for new models and systems, better ways to do things to push them through. [2]

This impeccably describes my experience with the guitar. No one naturally knows how to play the guitar, so at first I started out purposefully. I slowly and painfully learned one chord at a time. I painstakingly turned dissonant noise into tolerable music.

Then it became natural and easy. It became enjoyable as a matter of fact. And ironically, as soon as it became more than just a chore, I stopped improving. I starting using the entrepreneurial approach and just repeated what I had already

1. Gary Keller, *The One Thing*, Bard Publishing, Copyright 2013, Pg. 179
2. Ibid., Pg. 180

learned over and over again. It wasn't until I started to use the purposeful approach again that I finally started improving again. As Keller notes:

> *Too many people reach a level where their performance is 'good enough' and then stop working on getting better. People on the path to mastery avoid this by continually upping their goal, challenging themselves to break through their current ceiling, and staying the forever apprentice.* [3]

We all have things we are naturally inclined towards and others we are not. I, for example, was naturally inclined toward the guitar because I love music. I am not naturally inclined toward computer programming. The mere concept of it bores me. So the key to finding a job or business that can become a career and a vocation is to find something we are naturally inclined toward. But that is only the first step because it produces the incentive to fall into our natural state. However, in our natural state, we cannot reach mastery, only mediocrity.

Robert Greene makes the case that in order to achieve mastery, one must become an apprentice of the masters in that field and "…the goal of [this] apprenticeship is not money, a good position, a title, or a diploma, but rather a transformation of your mind and character." [4] Personal transformations do not happen naturally.

I can all but guarantee that several parts of your life or career have fallen into a natural autopilot. In our real estate

3. Gary Keller, *The One Thing*, Bard Publishing, Copyright 2013, Pg. 181-182
4. Robert Greene, *Mastery*, Penguin Books, Copyright 2012, Pg. 55

business as a whole, we had been slow with turning over units after tenants left because our maintenance staff already had their hands full, and our remodeling projects have taken the priority of our rehab staff. But this doesn't make any sense; rehabs take longer than turnovers so we're leaving money on the table.

At the same time, we can't just fix the problem by snapping our fingers because there is a risk in losing focus by bouncing employees from rehab projects to turnovers and then back again over and over. The whole situation is less than ideal, yet it was a natural process that came about because the rehab projects are more "sexy" and don't come up as erratically. So we decided to make turnover a priority and bring someone on staff specifically for turnover who would supplement maintenance or rehab as needed, not the other way around.

And as far as my personal life goes, well, I want to skip "leg day" just as much as the next guy.

23

Twenty Mile Marching Amidst Shiny Objects

Jim Collins has dedicated his life to understanding what makes companies great. In his book *Great by Choice*, Collins looks at which companies thrive and which do not under volatile market conditions. One of his major findings is that companies that were consistent in their approach did substantially better than those that took an erratic approach, either trying to jump ahead quickly or hunker down.

He calls it "20 mile marching" after the philosophy of expedition leader Ronald Amundsen. In 1911, Amundsen and his team faced off against Robert Falcon Scott in a quest to be the first people to ever reach the South Pole. Amundsen's team won. Scott's team not only lost—they didn't survive.

According to Collins, what separated them was Amundsen's almost dogmatic approach to preparation. As Amundsen said,

> *Victory awaits him who has everything in order –*
> *luck people call it. Defeat is certain for he who has*
> *neglected to take necessary precautions in time;*
> *this is called bad luck.* [1]

1. Jim Collins, *Great by Choice*, HarperBusiness, Copyright 2011, Pg. 13

But it wasn't just dogmatic preparation; it was "fanatic discipline." Namely,

> *Amundsen adhered to a regime of consistent progress, never going too far in good weather, careful to stay far away from the red line of exhaustion that could leave his team exposed, yet pressing ahead in nasty weather to stay on pace. Amundsen throttled back his well-tuned team to travel between 15 and 20 miles per day... When a member of Amundsen's team suggested they could go faster, up to 25 miles a day, Amundsen said no.* [2]

Needless to say, Robert Falcon Scott had no such discipline.

Jim Collins then applies the analogy to business, and I think it could just as easily be applied to life in general,

> *The 20 Mile March is more than a philosophy. It's about having concrete, clear, intelligent and rigorously pursued performance mechanisms that keep you on track. The 20 Mile March creates two types of self-imposed discomfort: **1.** the discomfort of unwavering commitment to high performance in difficult conditions, and **2.** the discomfort of holding back in good conditions.* [3]

2. Jim Collins, *Great by Choice*, HarperBusiness, Copyright 2011, Pg. 61
3. Ibid., Pg. 45

One example of such discipline is Southwest Airlines. They would open just a couple new cities each year, no matter how good the market was. In 1996, more than 100 cities wanted Southwest to open there; instead, they opened just four new locations—and they had an unbelievable 30 consecutive profitable years to show for it! Even after 9/11, when the airline industry was in shambles, Southwest still made a profit.

On the other side of the equation, Collins notes the failure of those who bounce around from thing to thing in his book *How the Mighty Fall*,

> *In December of 1980, Bank of America surprised the world with its new CEO pick... a vigorous forty-one-year-old... who told The Wall Street Journal that he believed the bank needed a good "kick in the fanny." Seven months after taking office, Samuel Amracost bought discount brokerage Charles Schwab... Then he engineered the largest interstate banking acquisition to date in the nation's history, buying Seattle-based Seafirst Corp. He launched a $100 million crash program to blast competitors in ATMs... Amracost ripped apart outmoded traditions, closed branches, and ended lifetime employment. He instituted more incentive compensations...* [4]

And on and on and on. The result?

> *Bank of America fell from its net income peak of*

4. Jim Collins, *How the Mighty Fall*, HarperCollins Publishers, Copyright 2009

*$600 million into a decline that culminated from
1985 to 1987 with some of the largest losses up to
that point in banking history.* [5]

What this illustrates the importance of taking a slow but
steady approach. After all, the tortoise beat the hare.

It also means that we should avoid being a jack of all trades
and a master of none.

In Collins most famous book, *Good to Great*, he looked at
11 companies whose stocks performed at or below the market for 15 years before a transition, which saw them beat the
market for 15 consecutive years by at least a factor of three.
He then compared those companies to 11 similar firms that
made no such transition. One of his team's key discoveries was
what he phrased "The Hedgehog Concept." The term comes
from Isaiah Berlin's essay, "The Hedgehog and the Fox." As
Collins describes it,

*The fox knows many things, but the hedgehog
knows one big thing... Berlin extrapolated from
this little parable to divide people into two basic
groups: foxes and hedgehogs. Foxes pursue many
ends at the same time and see the world in all its
complexity. They are "scattered or diffuse, moving
on many levels"... never integrating their thinking
into one overall concept or unifying vision. Hedgehogs, on the other hand, simplify a complex world*

5. Ibid.

into a single organizing idea, a basic principle or
concept that unifies and guides everything. [6]

In plain English, the great companies Collin's studied implemented The Hedgehog Concept, whereas the not-so-great companies acted like foxes. One example is Walgreens (a hedgehog) which drove fanatically to create convenient drugstores and nothing more. They went so far as to close down a Walgreen's store in a good location and open a new store "if a great corner location would open up just half a block away" since corner lots allowed customers to "enter and exit from multiple directions," [7] and were thereby the most convenient. CVS seems to have their own Hedgehog concept as well; which is to plop a store right next to Walgreens every time a new Walgreens opens.

But I digress, the comparison company Collins used for Walgreen's was Eckerd, who by contrast, "...compulsively leapt at opportunities to acquire clumps of stores – forty two units here, thirty six there, in hodgepodge fashion with no obvious unifying theme," [8] while also throwing itself into the home video market and other industries. Walgreens flourished, while Eckerd floundered.

John Maxwell discusses the same thing in his book *The 21 Irrefutable Laws of Leadership*. Rule 17 is the Rule of Prioritization, and he notes how Jack Welch took GE to unprecedented heights when he made the company focus on what it

---

6. Jim Collins, *Good to Great*, HarperCollins Publishers, Copyright 2001, Pg. 90-91
7. Ibid., Pg. 92
8. Jim Collins, *Good to Great*, HarperCollins Publishers, Copyright 2001, Pg. 93

was best at, rather than dabble in a little bit of everything. As Maxwell notes,

> *When Welch assumed leadership of GE in 1981, it was a good company. It had a ninety year history, the company stock traded at $4 per share, and the company was worth about $12 billion, eleventh best on the stock market. It was a huge, diverse company that included 350 strategic businesses. But Welch believed the company could become better. What was his strategy? He used the Law of Priorities.* [9]

Jack Welch decided to cut out every business line that couldn't meet one simple criterion; to be either the best or second best in the world at it. Of the 348 businesses or products lines he started with, all but 14 were either closed down or sold. And the result?

> *Since [Welch] took over, GE's stock has experienced a 2 to 1 split four times. And it trades at more than $80 per share as I write this [in 1998]. The company is currently ranked as the nation's most admired company according to Fortune, and it has recently become the most valuable company in the world, with a market capitalization of more than $250 billion.* [10]

9. John C. Maxwell, *The 21 irrefutable Laws of Leadership*, Thomas Nelson, Inc., Copyright 2007, Pg. 181-182
10. John C. Maxwell, *The 21 irrefutable Laws of Leadership*, Thomas Nelson, Inc., Copyright 2007, Pg. 182

In Pixar's wonderful film *Up*, the main characters find themselves amongst dogs who have collars that translate their thoughts into English. The thoroughly insightful dog Doug then explains to them how "my name is Doug" and he has "a good and smart master who made this collar so I can talk" and then "*SQUIRREL!*"[11]

Doug immediately loses track of what he's talking about and stares off camera at the squirrel for several seconds before returning his attention to our protagonists. And this joke is repeated throughout the movie to great effect.

Life is full of squirrels or shiny objects as I like to put it. These shiny objects could be a new entrepreneurial opportunity that's completely different than the one your pursuing, an attractive girl or boy who just happens to start flirting with you despite your Facebook relationship status, a job offer from a different company, the bright idea to learn a new language or instrument or some late-night infomercial selling whatever. These are shiny objects.

I don't mean to say that none of these are worth pursuing. But all of them cannot be simultaneously pursued. To master any given thing or to even become good at it requires a lot of time and energy. And unless your intent is to have a harem, the same could be said of any good relationship. You have to pick judiciously.

Furthermore, you can't cheat. You're not going to become a legendary pianist overnight. Nor is your new business venture going to be a Fortune 500 IPO in a few months. Great success requires a consistent, diligent and focused approach.

11. *Up*, Pete Docter and Bob Peterson, Walt Disney Pictures and Pixar Animation Studios, 2009

In whatever you pursue, to do it right, you must "20 mile march" in order to get there while avoiding the constant stream of shiny objects lined up along both sides of the road.

Conclusion

I wish I could say I've taken my own advice. Sure, I have to one extent or another, but I'm by no means perfect. Awesomeness, it would seem, is not something we can ever truly achieve. Instead, it's an ideal to which we must strive for.

In this short book I hope I have illustrated some ways that can help you attain this worthwhile ideal. Indeed, from my own experience, it's an ebb and flow sort of affair. At times I'll feel like I've all but mastered it. Then I fall back down into a funk. Then I will rise again like the Phoenix from the ashes of mediocrity only to come back down once again.

But upon reflection, each time I get up, I get up from a higher plateau and reach a higher peak than I did before. When viewed this way, I can relax and not worry so much about my next inevitable descent. Falling down is no reason to get depressed. Remember, we only live once. So enjoy your life!

If the pursuit of awesomeness becomes so overwhelming as to actually impede your own happiness, then it becomes counterproductive. Awesomeness should increase your happiness. Happiness and awesomeness should be joined at the hip like two peas in a pod, not adversaries. You cannot conquer happiness any more than you can conquer awesomeness. Instead, happiness comes from enjoying the path, not the destination. Because if life is the path, then the only destination to reach is death. So if you think that "getting there" will make you happy, unfortunately, you will never be happy.

Instead, you should enjoy the path. But the path along the road toward of awesomeness is so much better than the road of mediocrity.

It is my sincerest hope that this book has aided you along that path.

About the Author

Andrew Syrios is a real estate investor and writer living in Kansas City, Missouri. He is a partner in Stewardship Investments, LLC alongside his brother Phillip and father Bill, which he joined after graduating from the University of Oregon. In addition, he writes for Thought Catalog and Bigger-Pockets as well as a variety of other websites from time to time. Finally, he is a part-time, amateur scholar in the study of awesomeness.

Thought Catalog, it's a website.

www.thoughtcatalog.com

Social

facebook.com/thoughtcatalog
twitter.com/thoughtcatalog
tumblr.com/thoughtcatalog
instagram.com/thoughtcatalog

Corporate

www.thought.is

www.ingramcontent.com/pod-product-compliance
Lightning Source LLC
Chambersburg PA
CBHW031535040426
42445CB00010B/545

* 9 7 8 0 6 9 2 6 7 8 1 3 8 *